AF478186

MINI CAR BIBLE

TECTUM
PUBLISHERS

CAR

MINI

BIBLE

© 2009   Tectum Publishers
Godefriduskaai 22
2000 Antwerp
Belgium
info@tectum.be
+ 32 3 226 66 73
www.tectum.be

ISBN: 978-90-79761-24-1
WD: 2009/9021/27
(90)

PHOTOGRAPHY : Reinhard Lintelmann
& Neill Bruce Picture Library
DESIGN : Gunter Segers

PREFACE

The automobile is celebrating its birthday. This extraordinary technical development has been with us for 125 years. When Karl Benz first introduced the "Benz Patent Motorwagen" - the world's first automobile - in 1886, he had no idea of the technical challenges his invention would be subjected to over time. Although the early motorcars were regarded somewhat skeptically as a mere alternative to horse-drawn carriages, it was soon apparent that they weren't just a means of conveyance. The endless demand for better performance and more comfort resulted in ever faster and more luxurious cars. They freed their passengers from the limitations of time and space, and their unceasing further development gave birth to an economically vital branch of industry. Whereas the legendary eight- and twelve-cylinder cars of the 1930s with their elegant bodies were largely the product of expensive hand crafting, some manufacturers were already recognizing the tremendous buyer potential to be realized through the more economical process of assembly line production. The automobile's appearance was soon being determined by new technologies in car body construction. By the 1950s, unique, custom-built car bodies were becoming less and less common, as the laws of aerodynamics and increased safety awareness were increasingly shaping and determining the uniform appearance of the majority of vehicles. Only a few smaller manufacturers, dedicated to producing high-class sports and luxury cars, continued to make automobiles that appealed to the rugged individualist. The demand for unusual one-offs and limited-series luxury-class automobiles is greater than ever before. Along with the classic cars of the past, these showpieces are the real eye-catchers on our streets. The desire for individualism that has colored automotive history from the very beginning will continue to ensure that both mass production and creativity find their proper place.
The Mini Car Bible showcases the creative genius of automotive manufacturers and designers and is dedicated to important makes and models of the past as well as to the stars of the present.

Reinhard Lintelmann
PHOTOGRAPHER WITH A PASSION FOR CARS

AC Autokraft Cobra Mk IV • Great Britain • 1991

GT·NM 4

Alfa Romeo 8C Competizione • Italy • 2007

ALFA ROMEO
8C Competizione

8C Competizione
8C Competizione

Alfa Romeo 8C Monza 2300 • Italy • 1931

FP
222

FP 222

Alpine A 110/1600 • France • 1968

ALPINE
OS·YY·11

Aston Martin DB6 • Great Britain • 1965

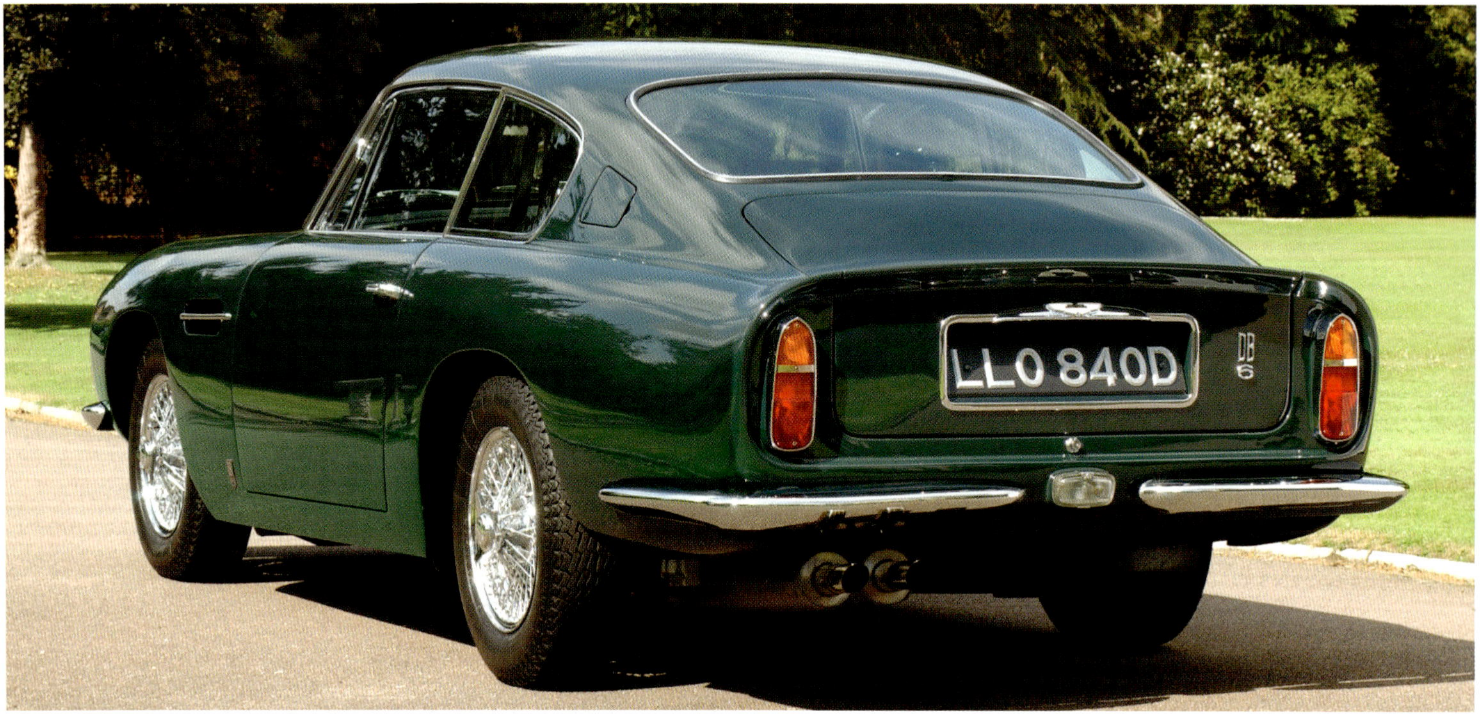

DAVID BROWN
ASTON MARTIN

SMITHS
FUEL
E 1/4 1/2 3/4 F
SMITHS
90 6 4
15844
20 40 60 80 100 120 140 160 180
HIGH BEAM
M P H
LUCAS
AMPS
50+
SMITHS
10 20 30 40
R P M
X100
6. CYL
POSITIVE EARTH
FUEL RESERVE
30 65 85 100 110

Auburn Speedster 851 • USA • 1934
SUPER-CHARGED

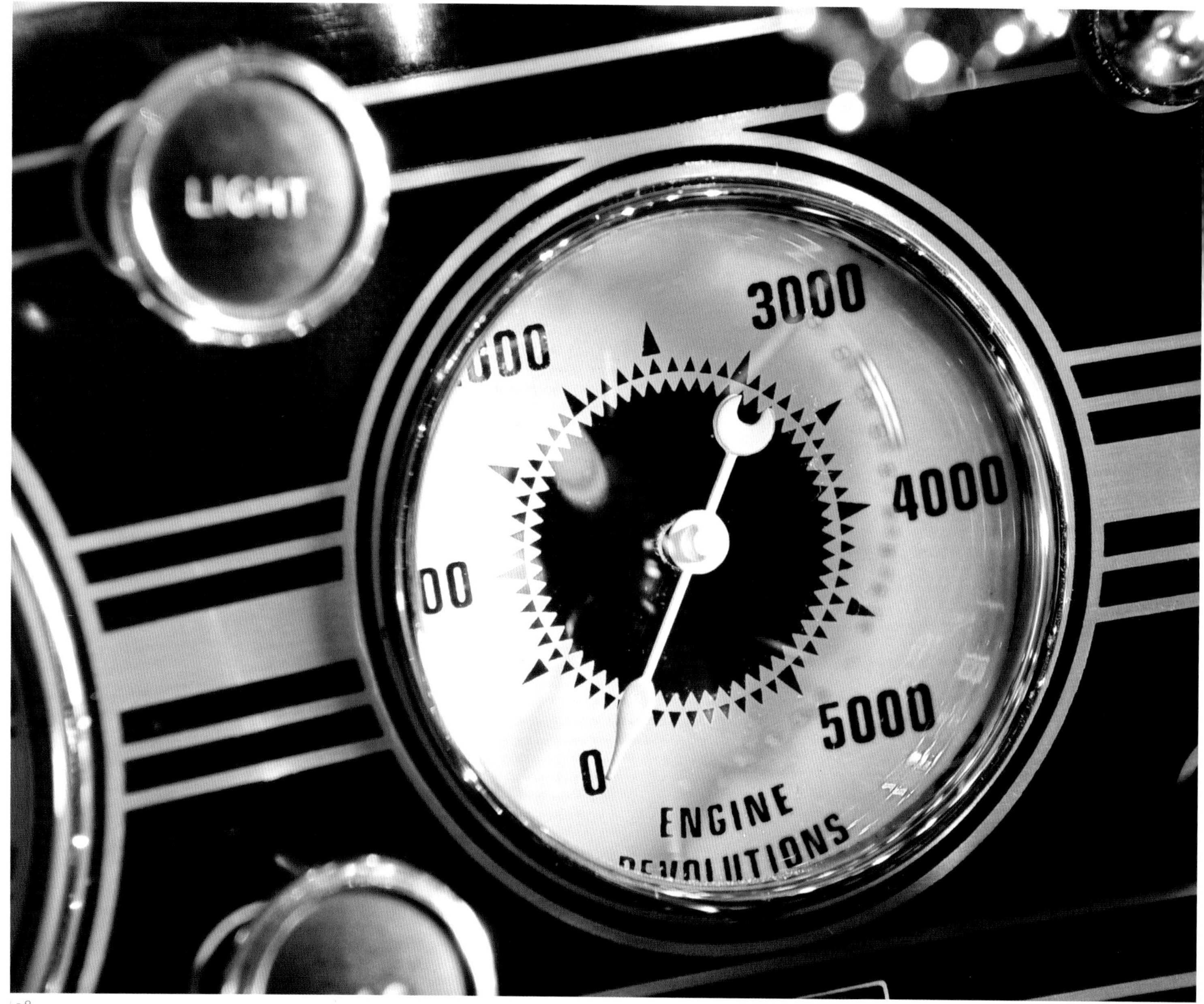

LIGHT
3000
600
4000
00
5000
0
ENGINE
REVOLUTIONS

Audi R8 • Germany • 2006

LLK 909
GB

Austin Healey 3000 MK III • Great Britain • 1964

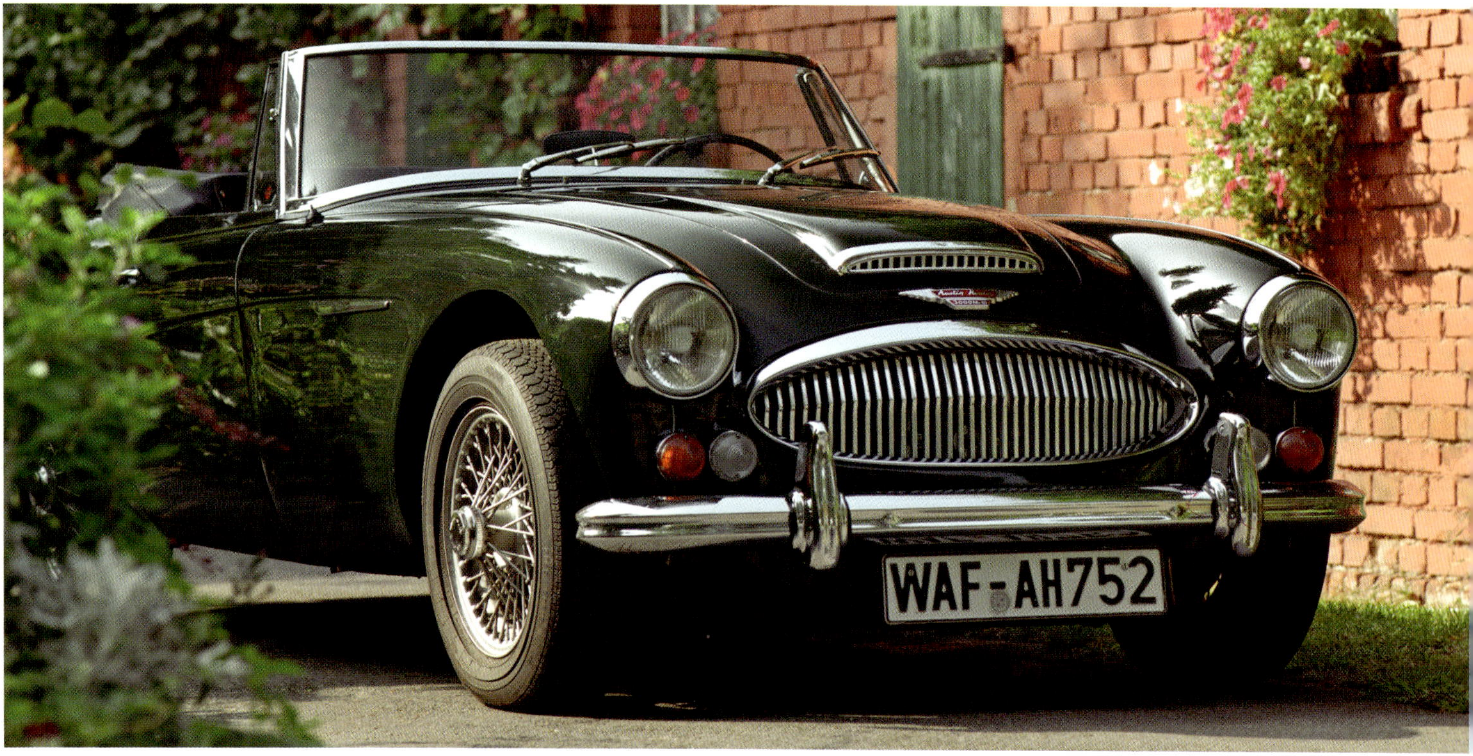

Austin Healey
3000 Mk III

WAF - AH752

Bentley 4 ½ Litre • Great Britain • 1927

BENTLEY

ANDRE
HARTFORD
SHOCK
ABSORBER
TYPE 50A
2
1
3
5
4

BENTLEY
OIL
OFF
ON
OFF
OPEN
THROTTLE
CLOSED
ADVANCED
IGNITION
RETARDED
JAEGER
DYNAMO
IN
OFF
BENTLEY MOTORS LTD LONDON
MIXTURE
RICH
WEAK
CHASSIS № U K 3279

ST - AR 868

Benz Patent Motorwagen • Germany • 1886

Bizzarrini GT 5300 Strada • Italy • 1966

BMW 328 • Germany • 1937

BMW 507 • Germany • 1955

BR 35777

BMW M1 • Germany • 1978

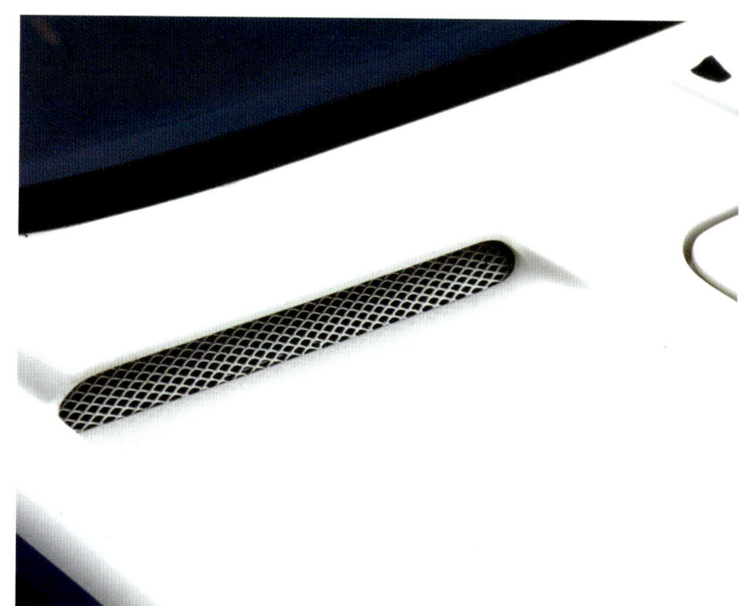

Bond Minicar Mk C • Great Britain • 1951

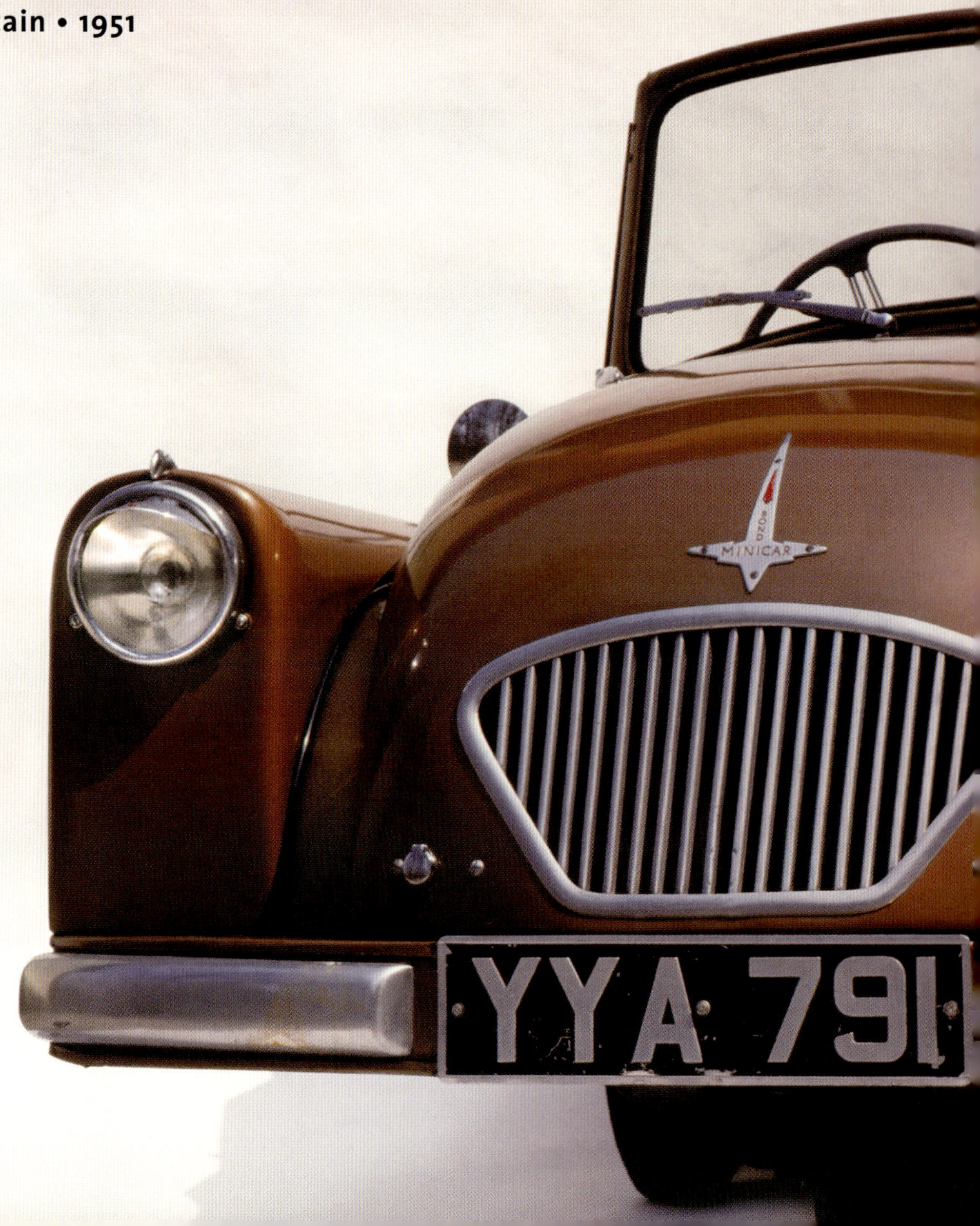

30
20 M.P.H. 40
10 50
X 42873/83
1300
60
3 1 8 5 7
SMITHS

Borgward Isabella Coupé • Germany • 1957

Borgward
OS-TL 161

RS-KY 7

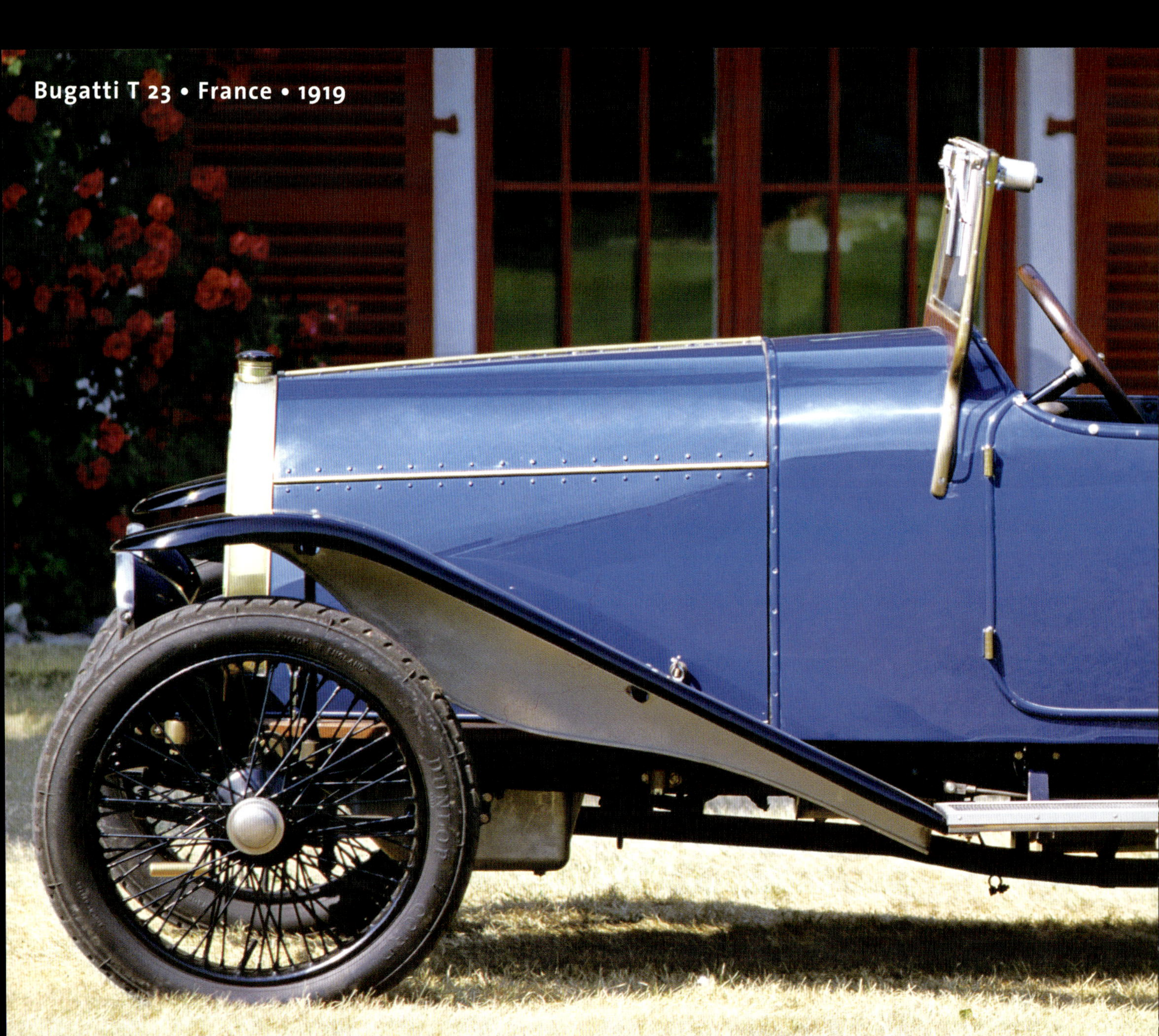
Bugatti T 23 • France • 1919

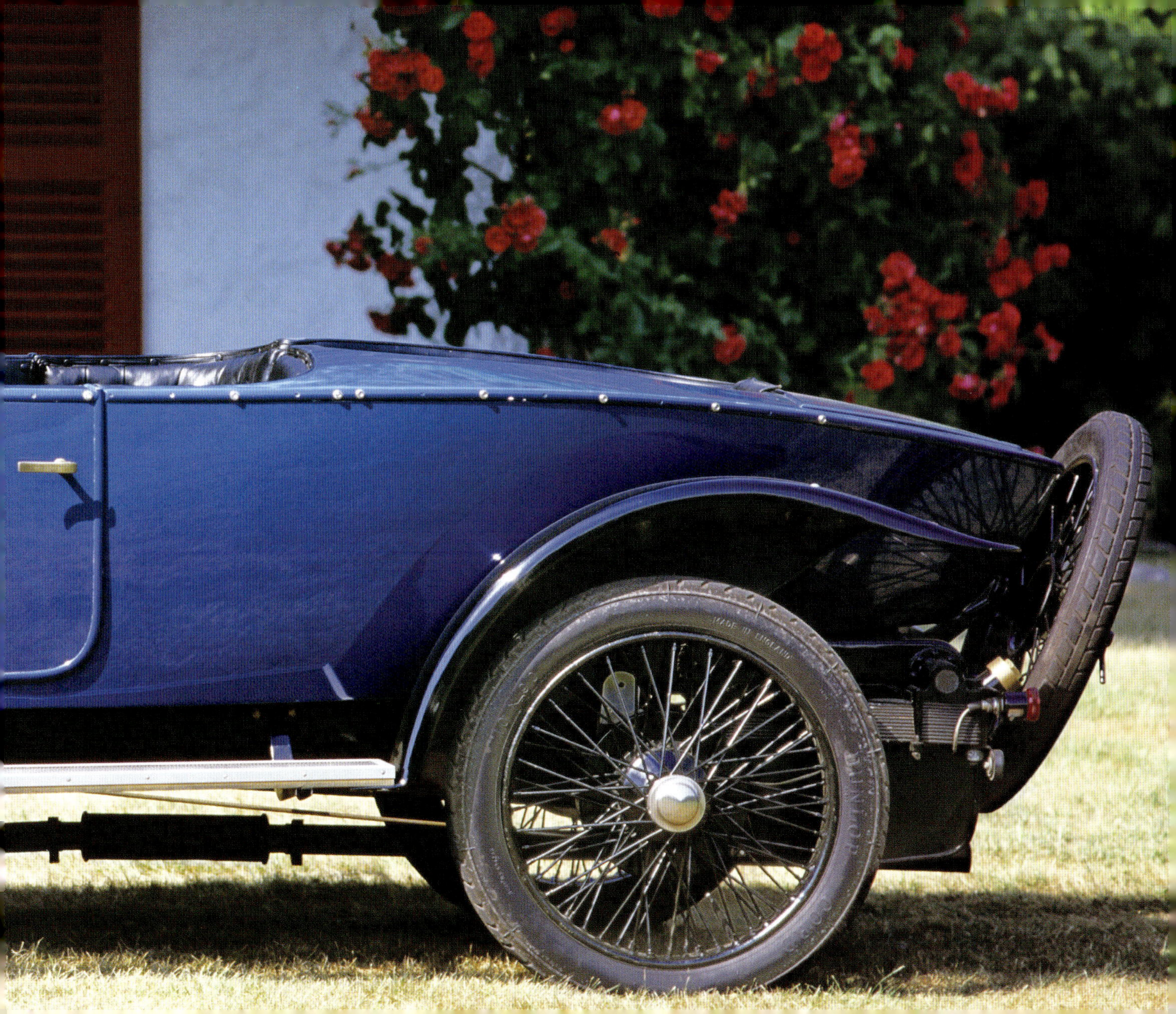

Bugatti T57 SC Atlantic • France • 1936

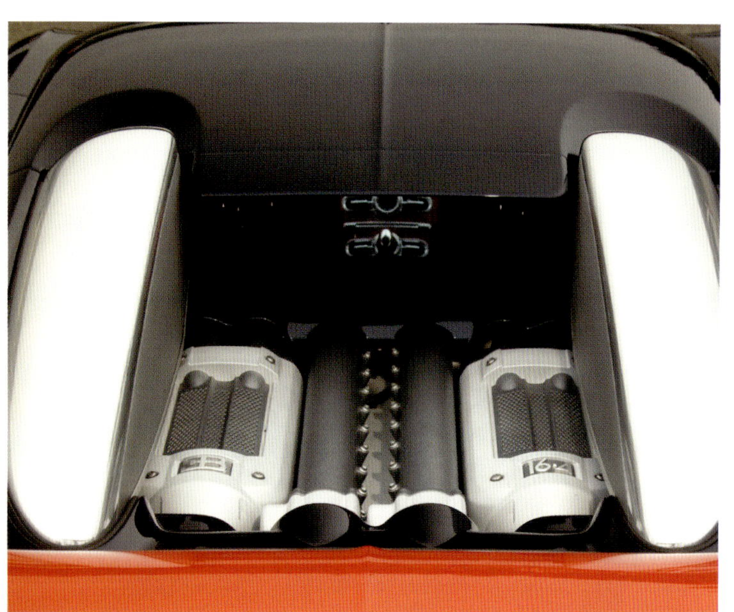

BUGATTI

Cadillac Eldorado Brougham • USA • 1959

0 20 40 60 80 100 120 140 160 180 220
C   H
TEMP
47421
FUEL
P   N   DR
VENTILATION
LEFT   OFF   ON
RIGHT   OFF   ON
DEFROSTER
COOL   DE-FOG   DE-ICE
WARMER
HEATER
12
3
6
9

CALIFORNIA
DSK 289
CADILLAC

Cadillac S 62 • USA • 1946

TS·V 4

Cadillac Sixteen V16 • USA • 1930

CADILLAC
MOTOR
CAR
CO.
16

CHEVROLET
Corvette

Citroen DS21 • France • 1968

MI-DS 19

MI · DS 19

Cord 812 • USA • 1937

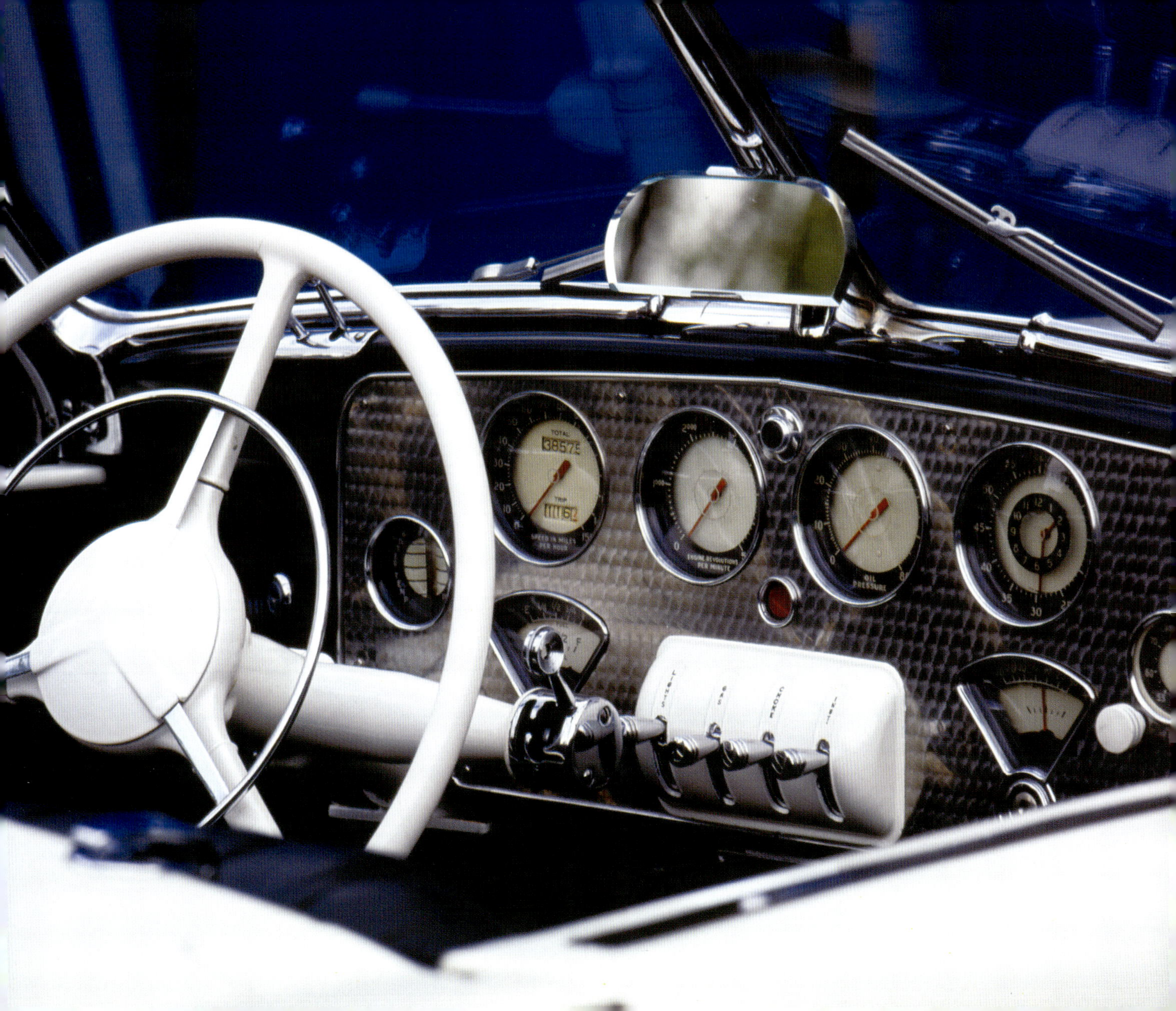

De Lorean DMC 12 • Great Britain • 1981

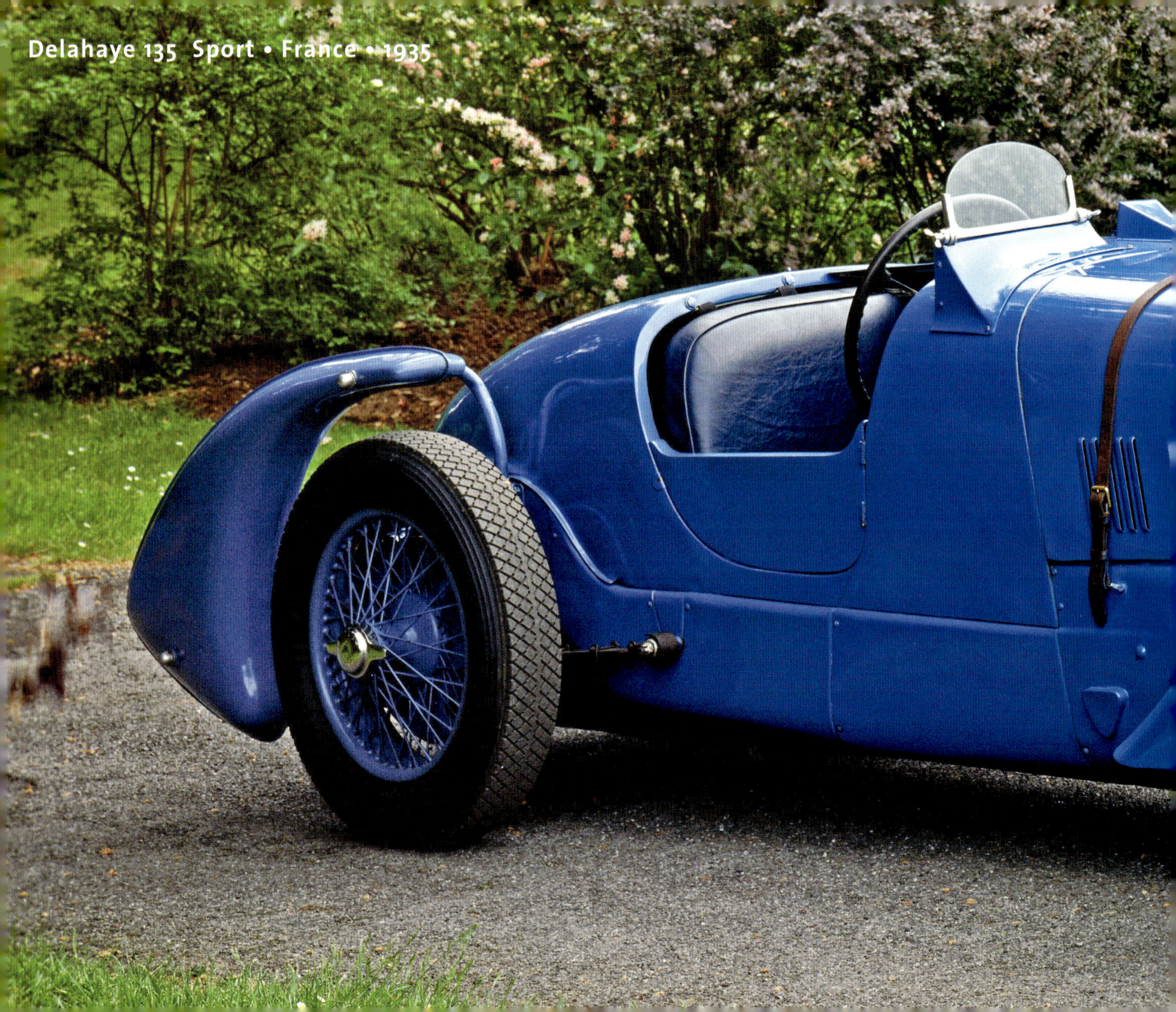
Delahaye 135 Sport • France • 1935

DUV 870

Dino 246 GT • Italy • 1969

Modena Motorsport
AC - J 222

Düsenberg SJ • USA • 1932

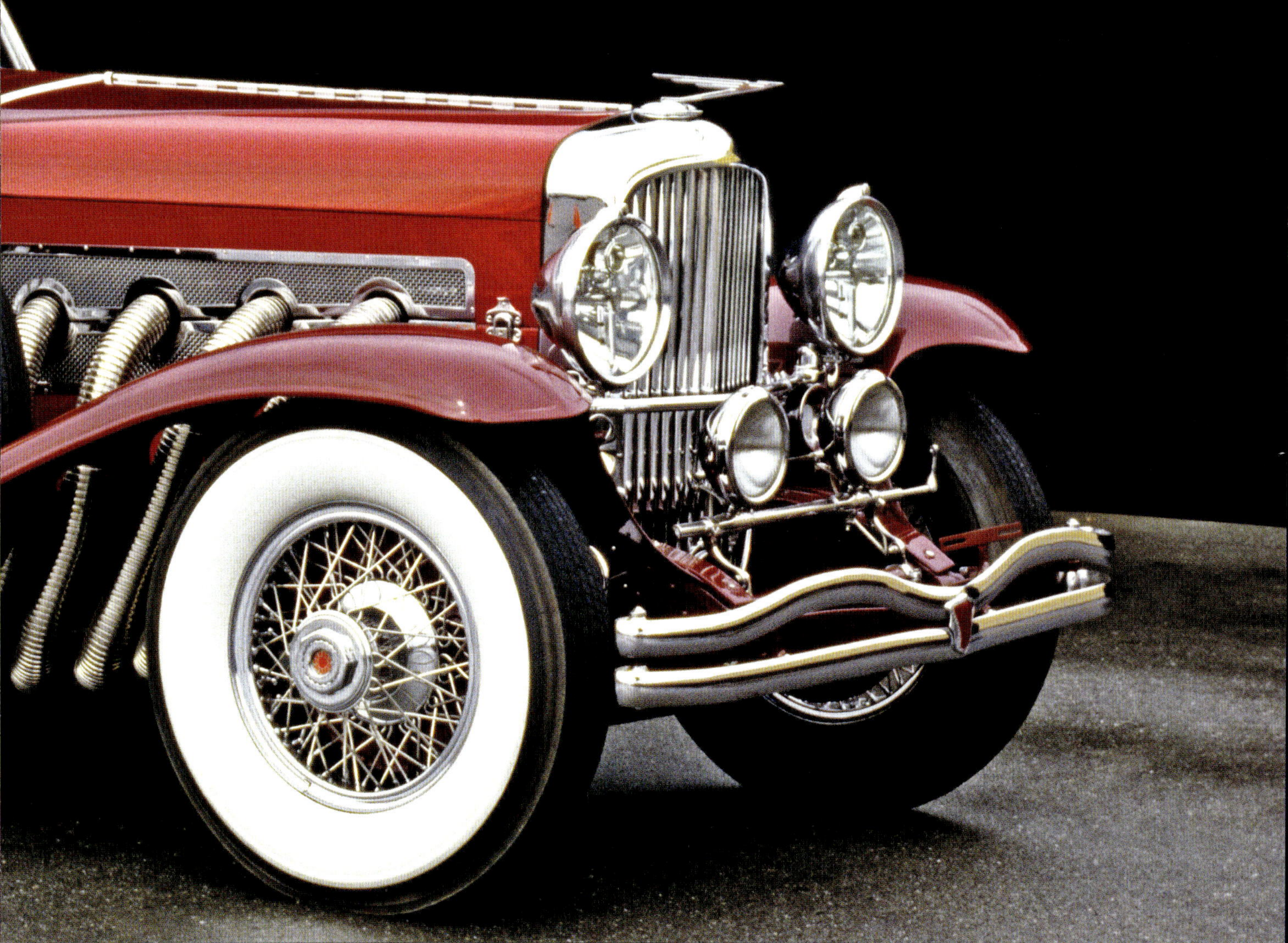

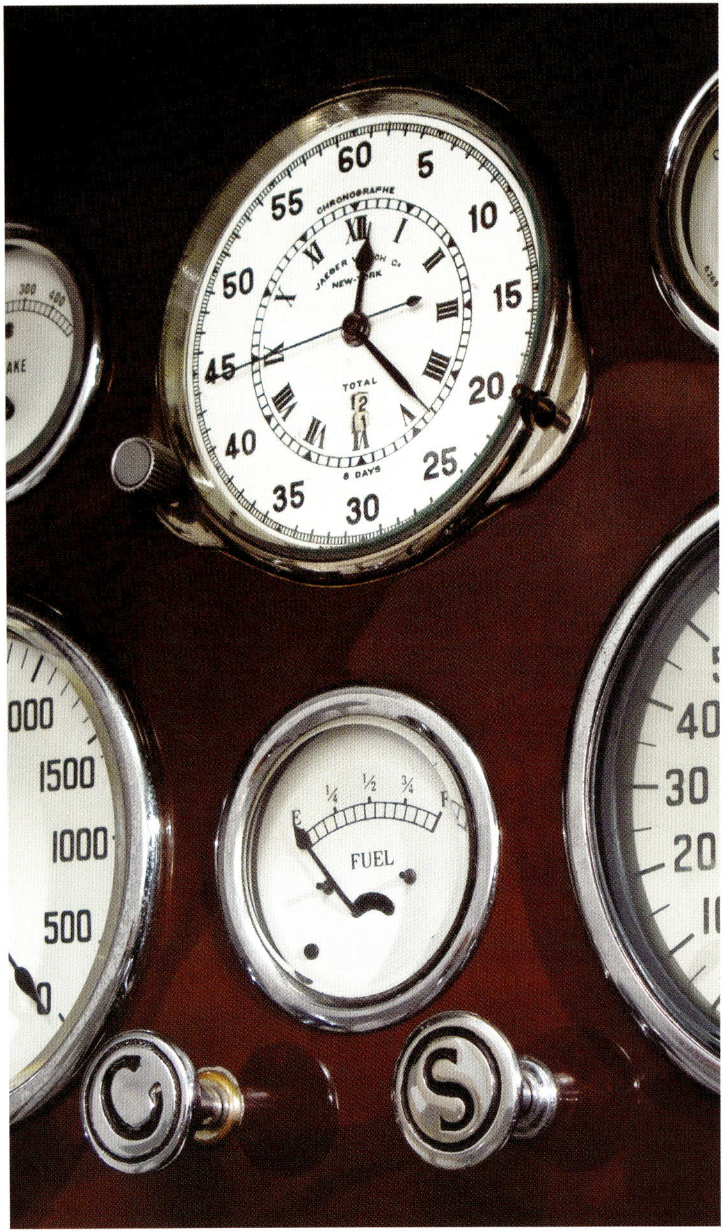
CHRONOGRAPHE
TOTAL
8 DAYS
FUEL

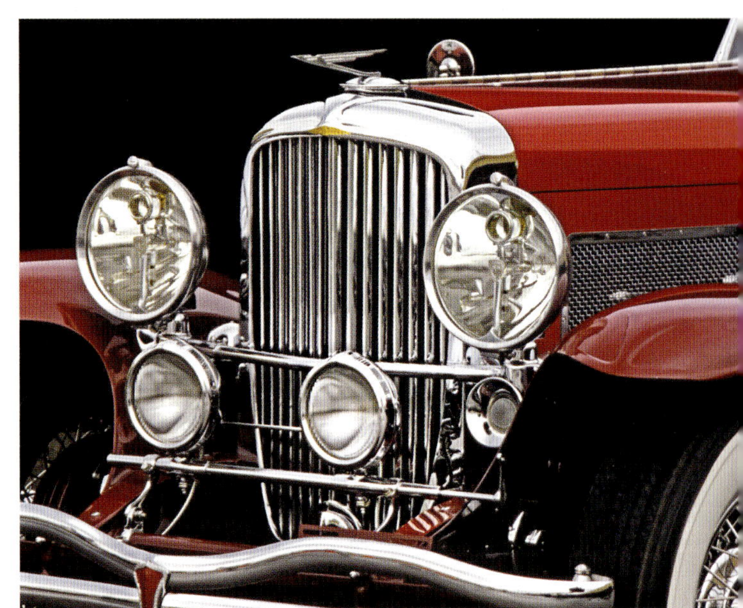

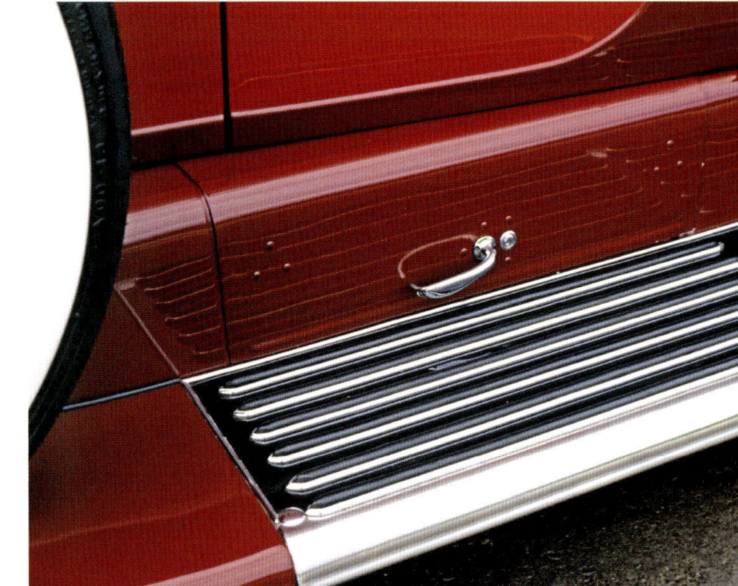

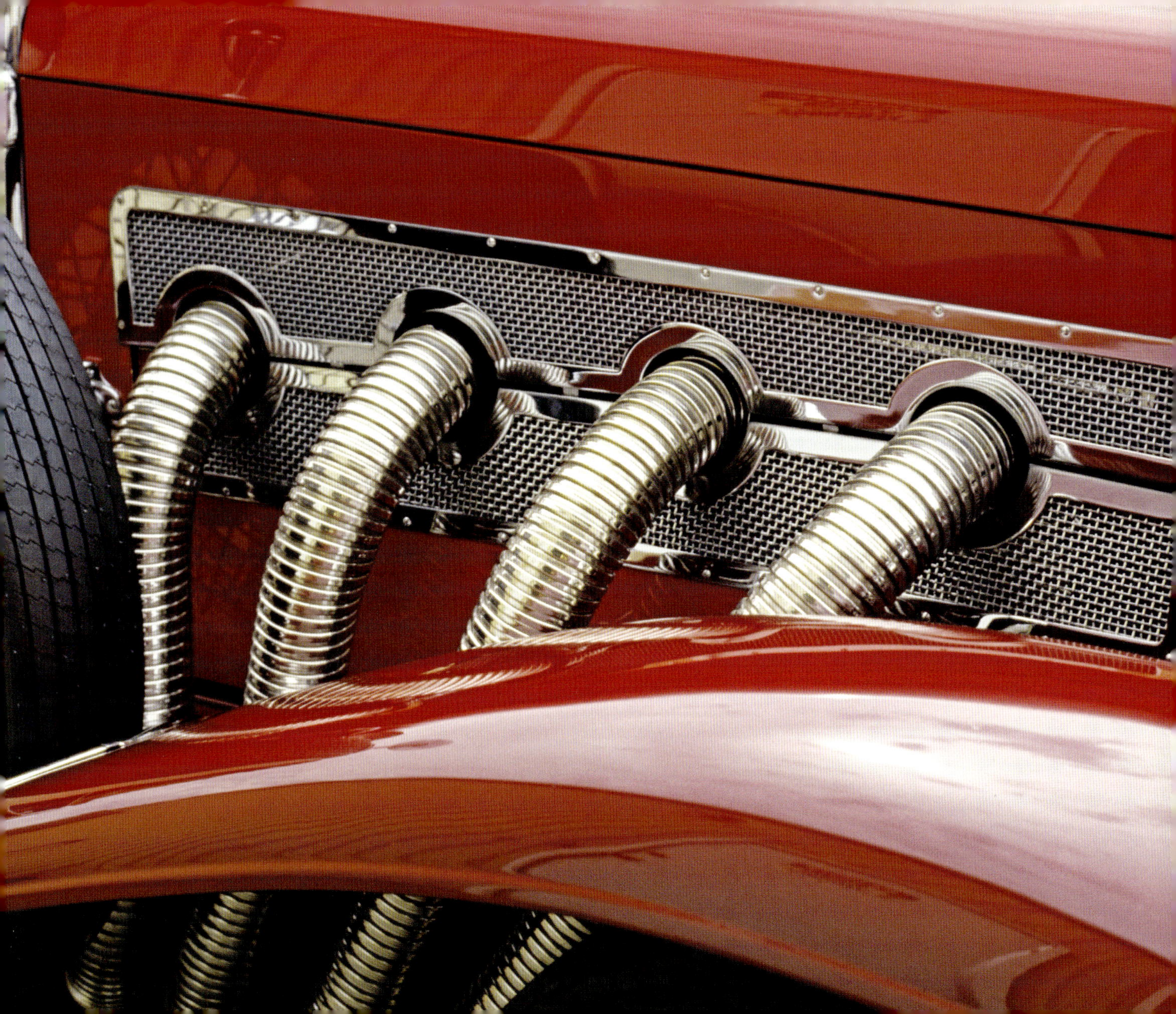

Ferrari 250 GTO • Italy • 1962

Ferrari 275 GTB / 4 N.A.R.T. Spider • Italy • 1966

MS-AY 111

Ferrari 500 TRC • Italy • 1957

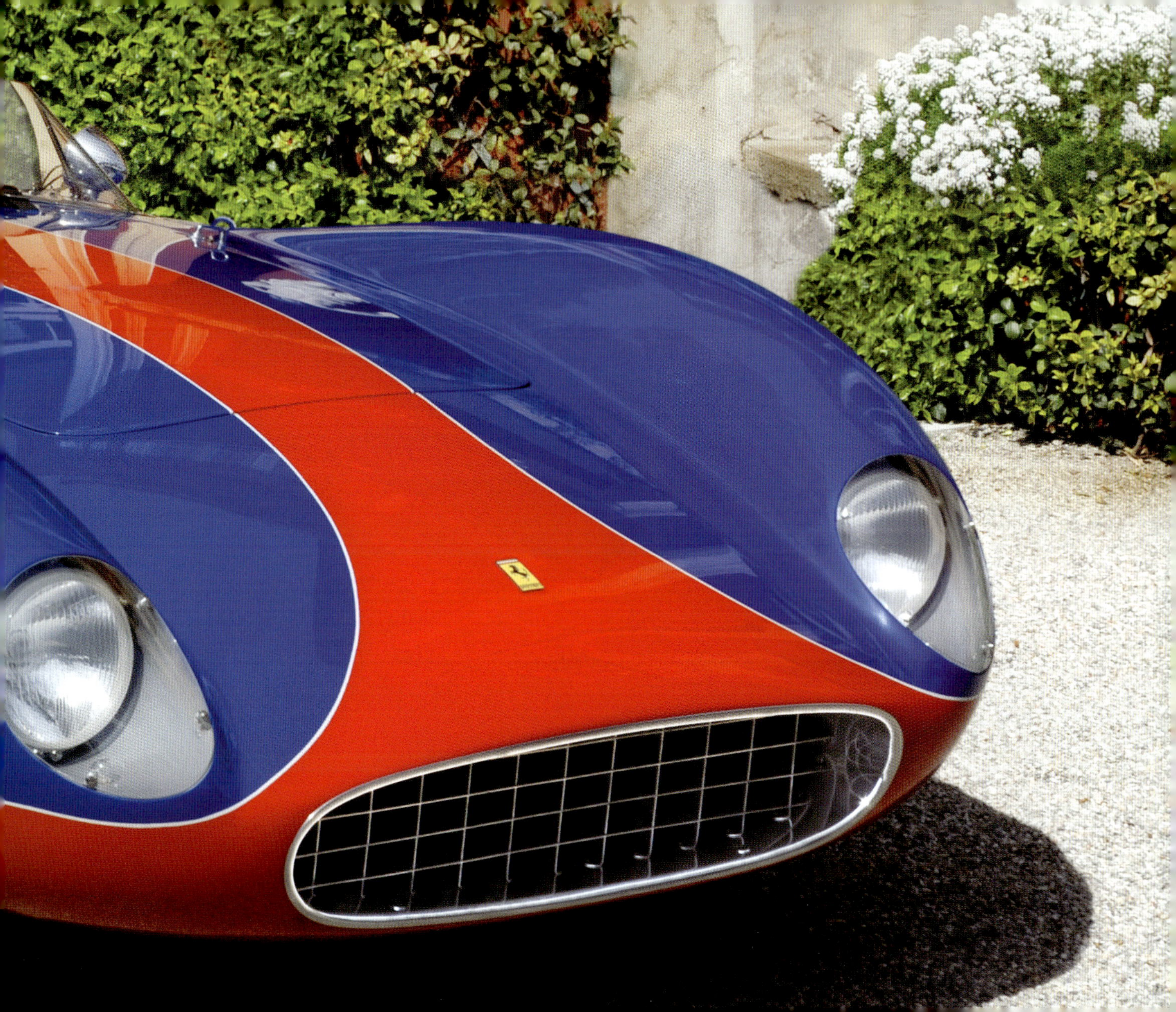

Kg/cm²
OLIO
SACMA-MILANO
10
20
30
40
50
60
70
80
90
100
JAEGER
GIRI x100
Ferrari
SACMA-MILANO
80
70
60
50
30
SACMA-MILANO

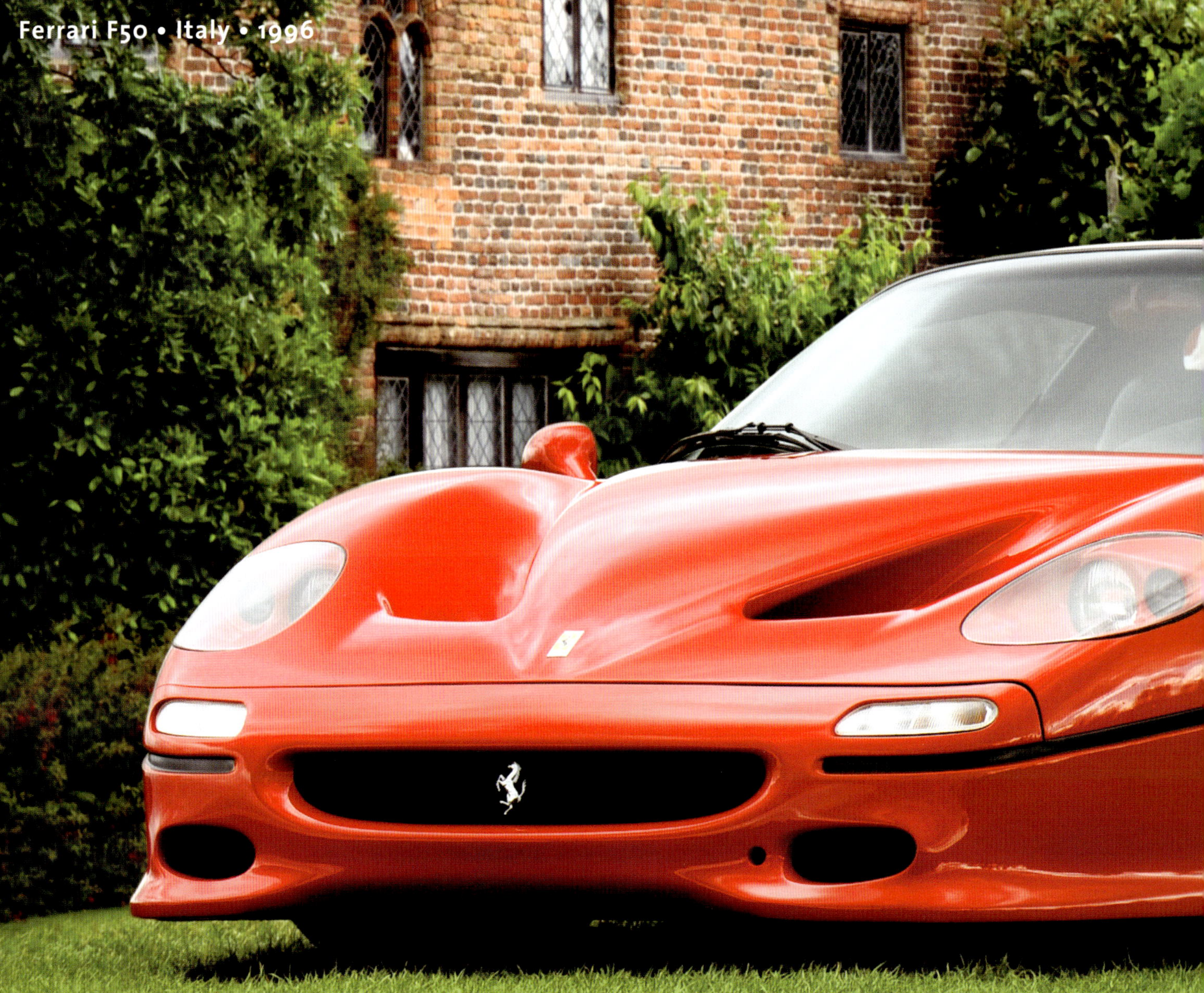
Ferrari F50 • Italy • 1996

J363

Ferrari

FZ09 TYW

AUR
C 7
D

Balilla
AUR·C 7

Ford Model T • USA • 1908

CALIFORNIA
TBC 316

CALIFORNIA
TBC 316

Ford Thunderbird • USA • 1955

SPORTSMAN'S PARADISE
262D141
LOUISIANA 91

MISSISSIPPI
5
1987

Horch 853 A • Germany • 1938

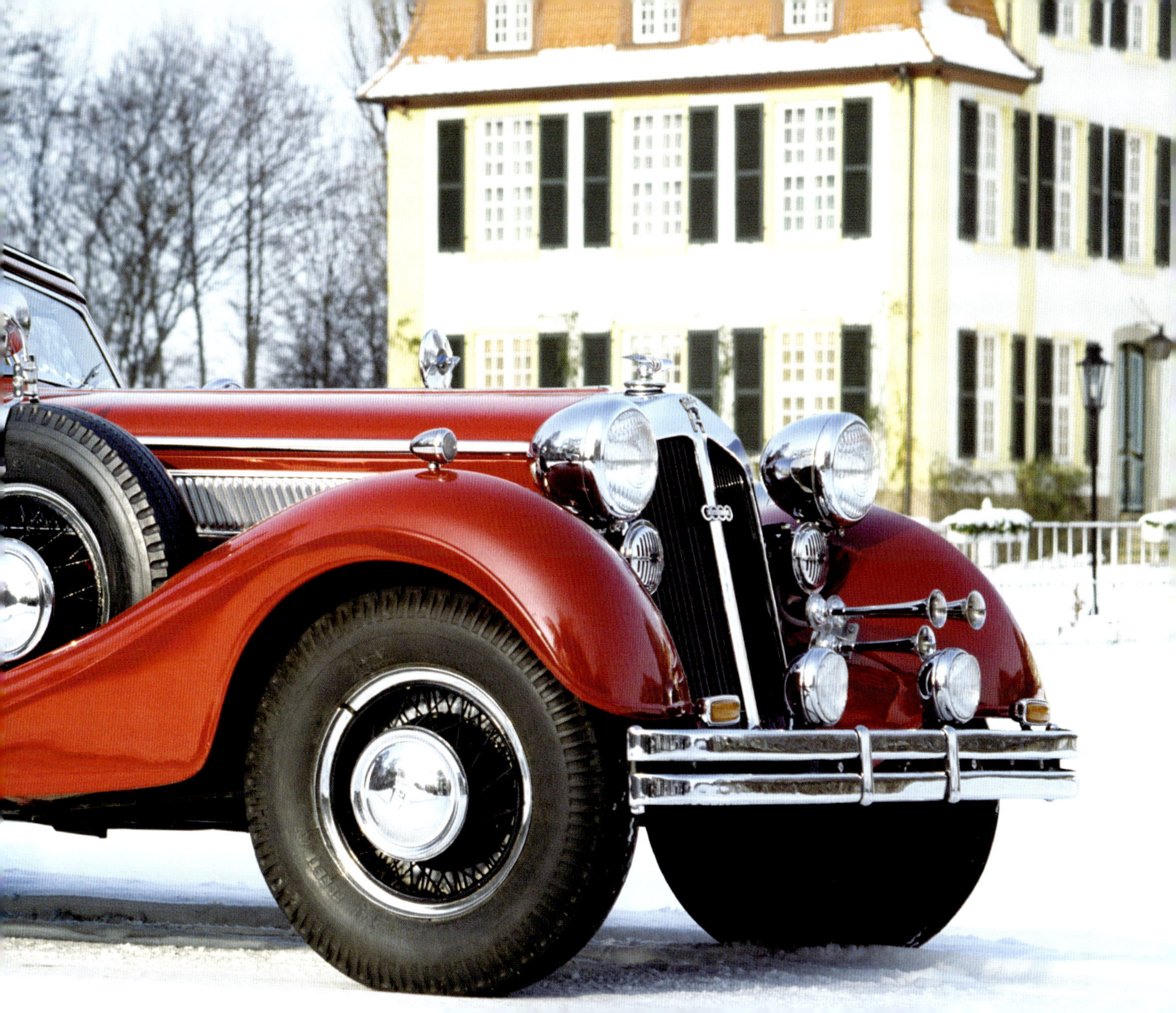

HORCH

160
140
120
100
80
60
40
20
0
54514
1000

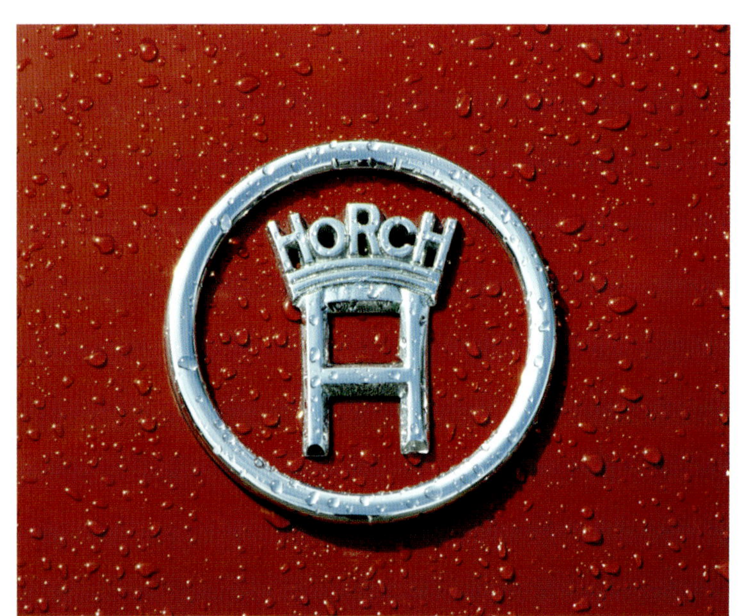

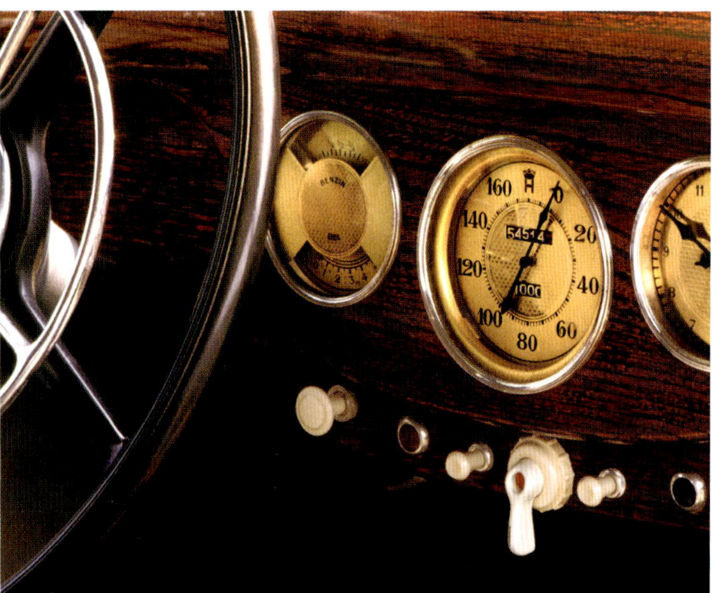

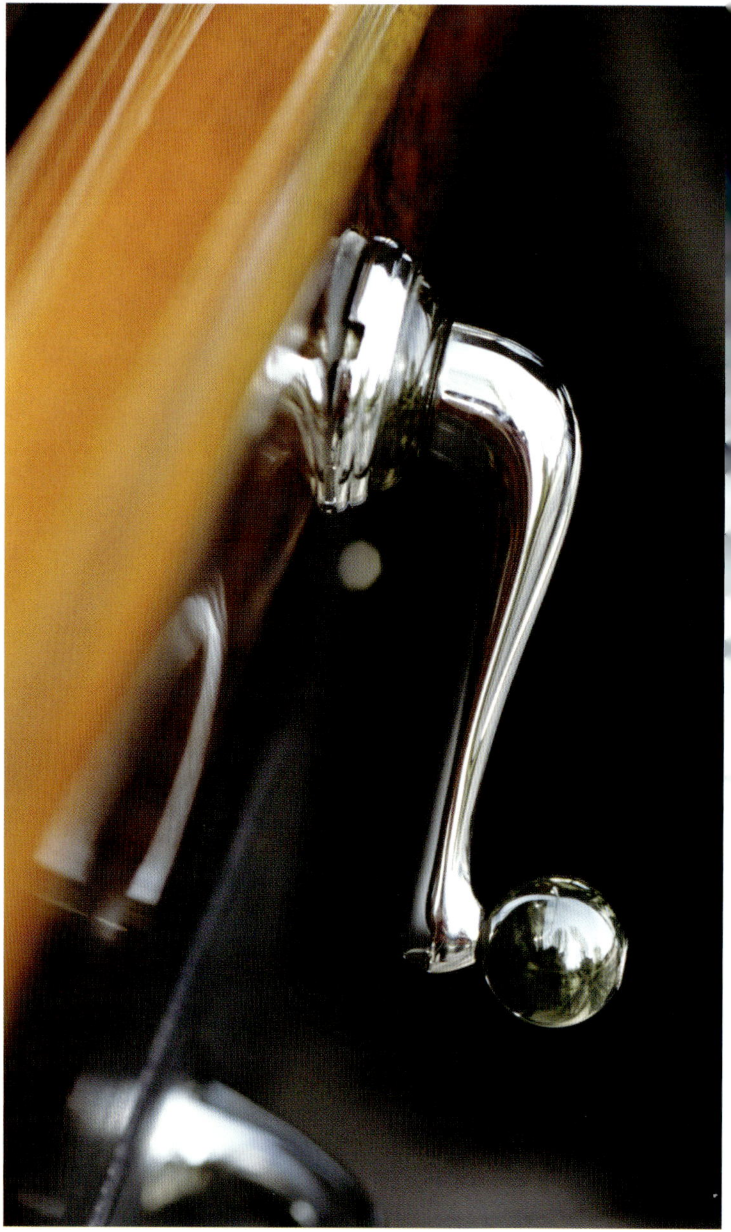

Jaguar E-Type S1 • Great Britain • 1961

K644 WJO

XJ220

JAGUAR
PREMIUM
UNLEADED

ST·JX 120

ST JX 120

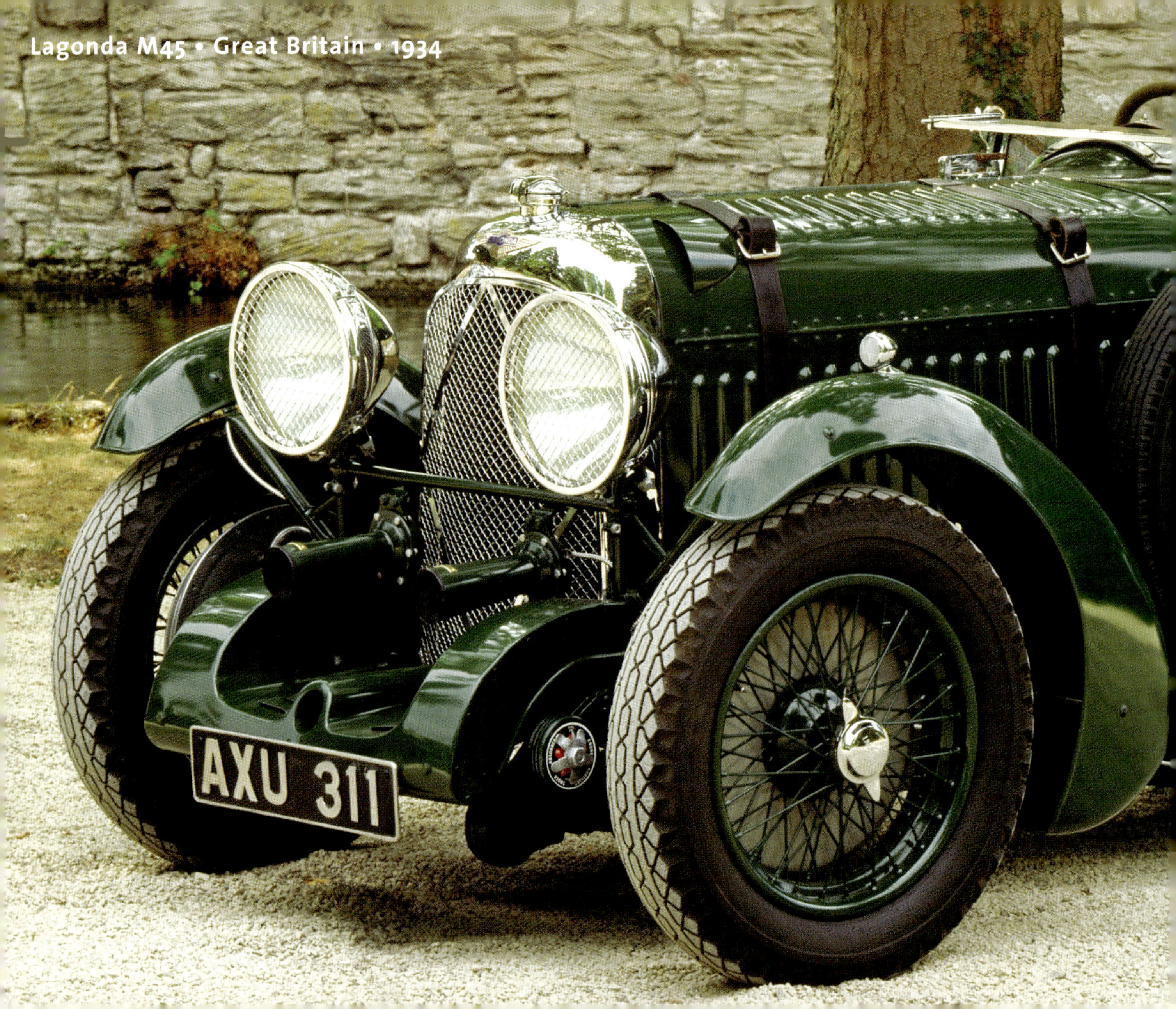
Lagonda M45 • Great Britain • 1934

LIMITED
STAINES ENGLAND
LAGONDA
OIL
LAGONDA
MILES
LAGONDA

Lamborghini Countach LP 400 • Italy • 1974

Lamborghini P 400 Miura • Italy • 1966

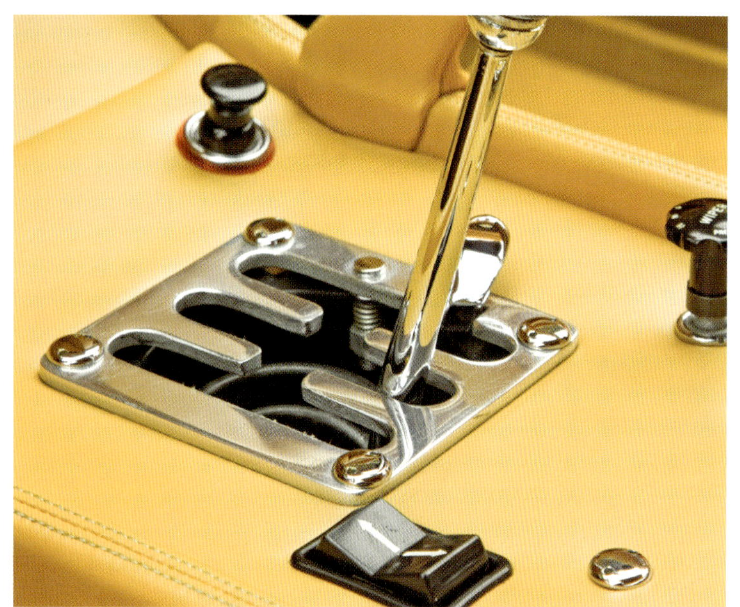

BERTONE
bertone
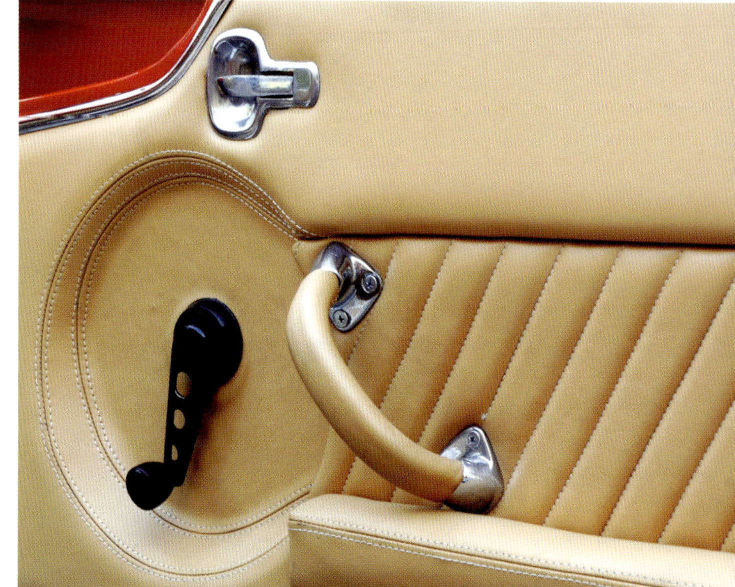

Lancia Aurelia B 20 GT • Italy • 1951

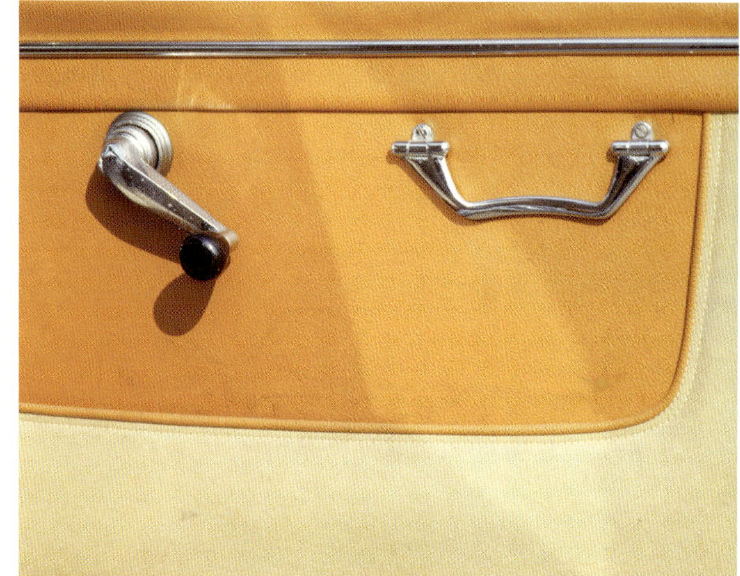

RPU 655M

Maserati Ghibli Coupé • Italy • 1966

DOJ 1C

MPH
38495
PRESS. OLIO
OIL PRESS
x 100

Maserati MC12 • Italy • 2004

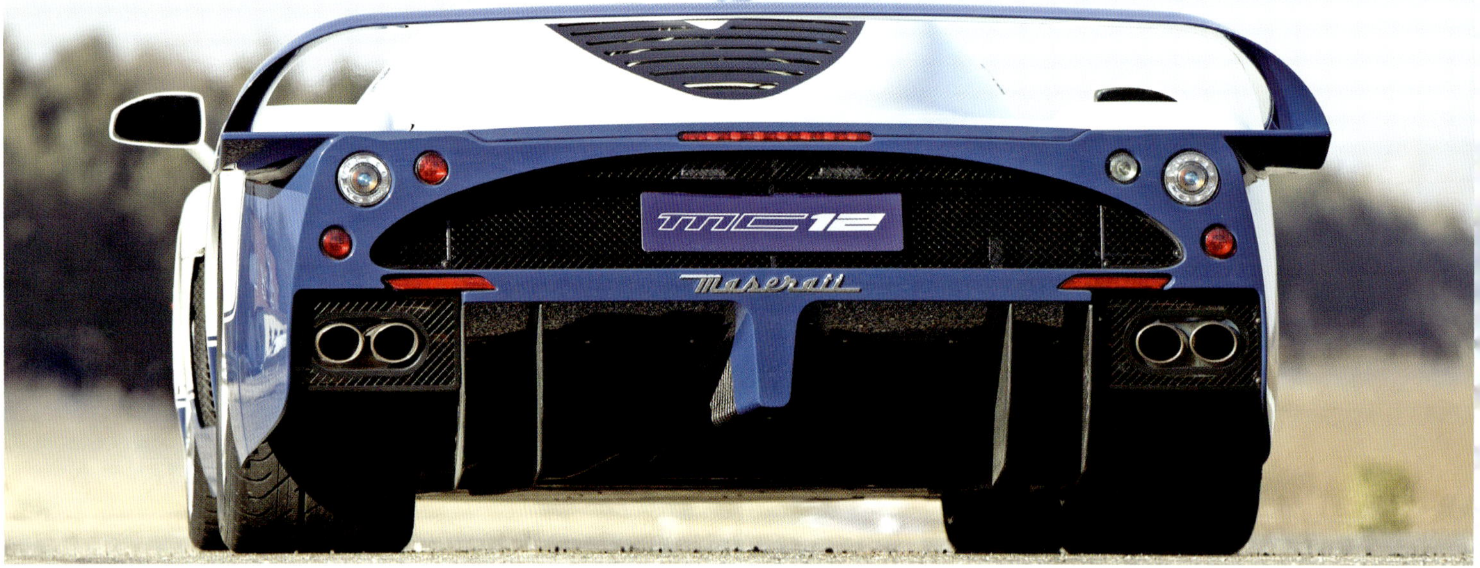
MC12
Maserati

0
1
2
3
4
aut
aut
22
24
20
26
18
STOP
Maserati

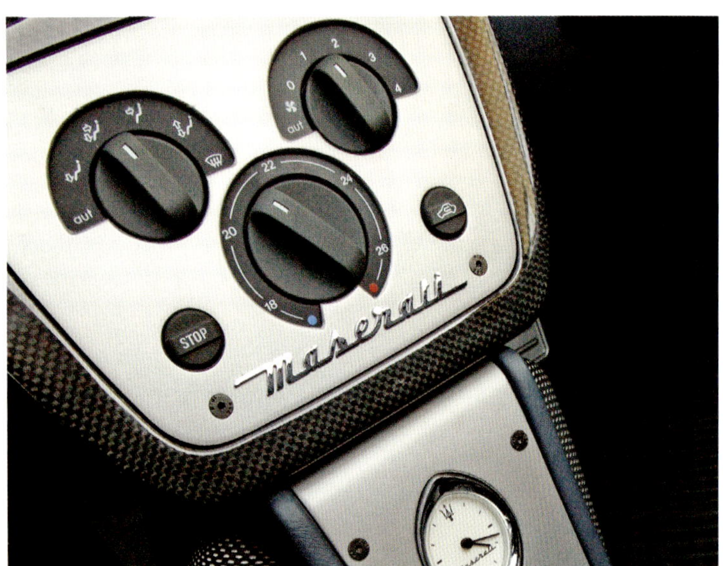

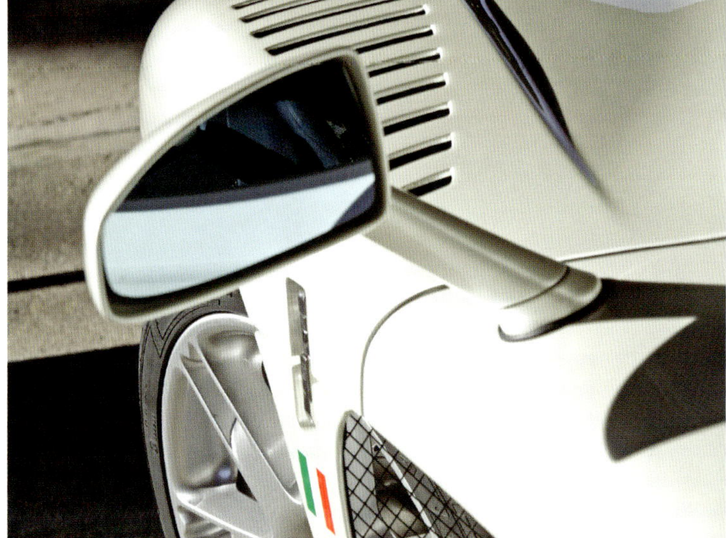

V12
24v
Maserati
rpm x 1000
bar
STOP
START
Maserati

S·MM 6231
62s

ZEPPELIN
7405 · JE 93

MAYBACH
7405 JE 93
F

Mercedes-Benz 300 SL Coupé • Germany • 1954

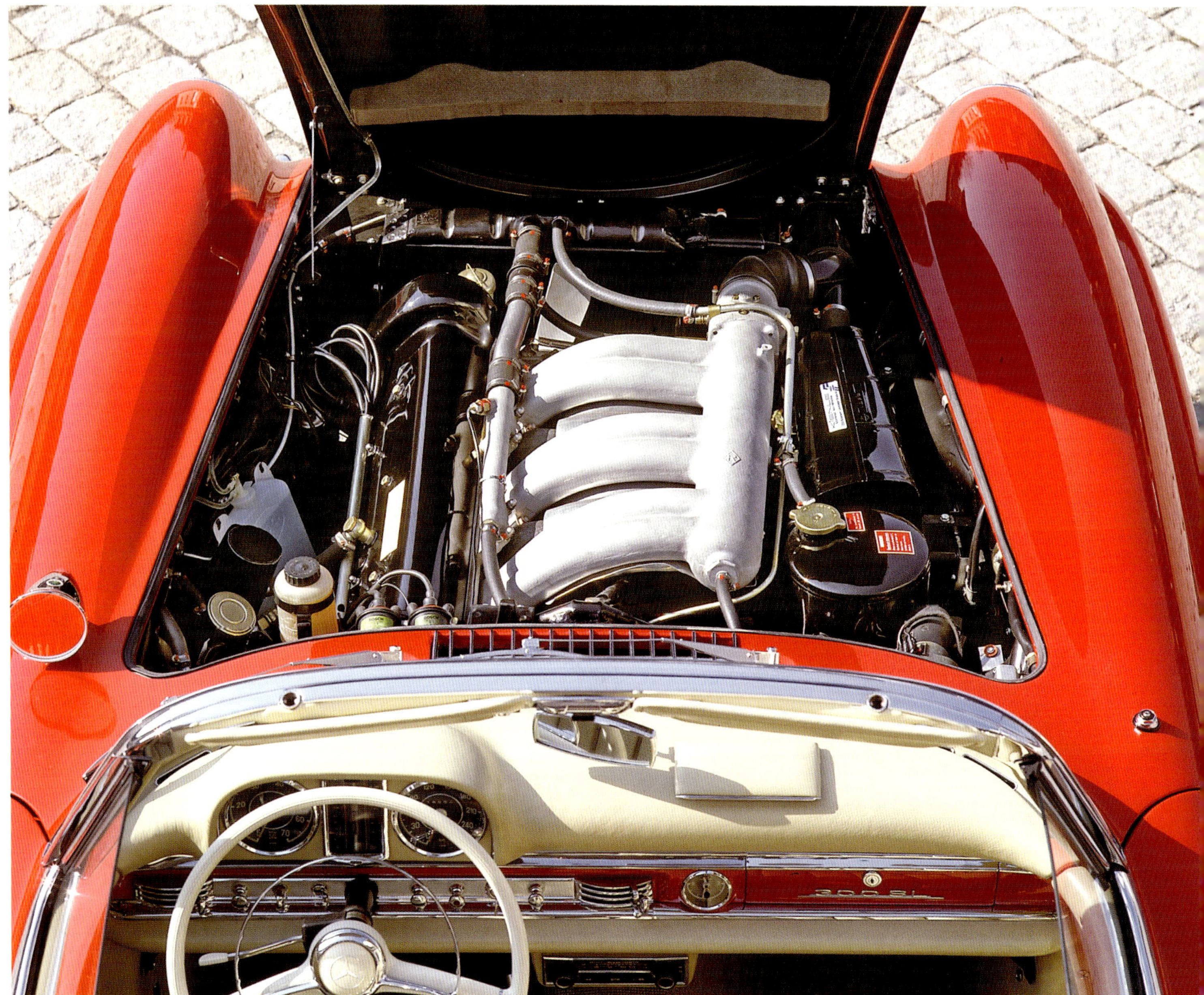

30
40
50
20
60
10
70
RPM
x 100
UPM
VDO
120
80
40
°C W.
4/4
3/4
1/2
1/4
RES
TANK
VDO
120
80
40
°C OEL
6
4
2
0
OEL/p
120
150
90
180
60
210
30
240
km
88638
VDO

Mercedes-Benz 540 K • Germany • 1936

Mercedes-Benz SLR McLaren • Germany • 2004

Mercedes-Benz SSK • Germany • 1930

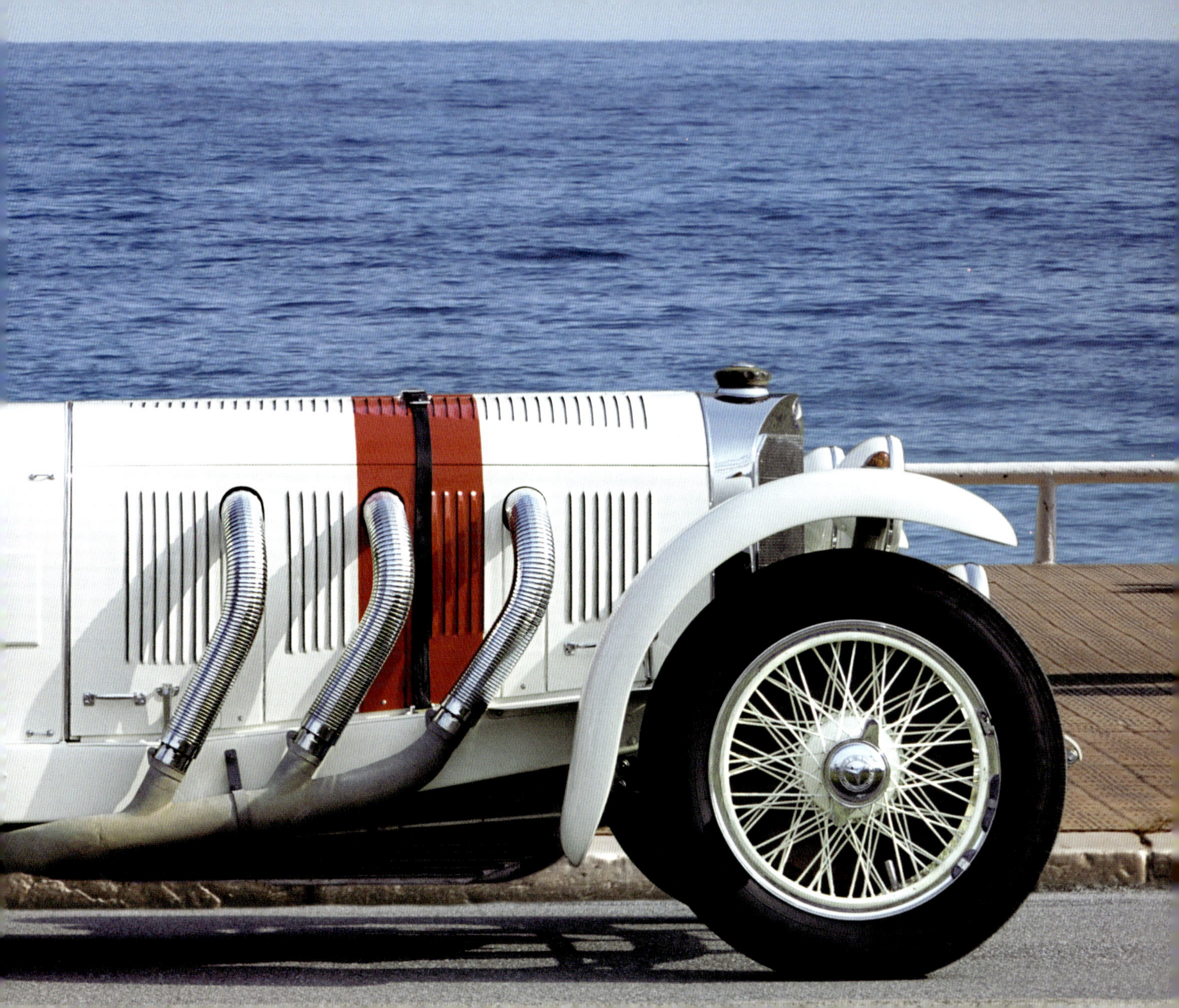

Mercedes Simplex • Germany • 1902

A.S.C
1905

60
70
50
MADE BY
S.SMITH & SON
40
80
263--7231
FOR
90
30
20
100

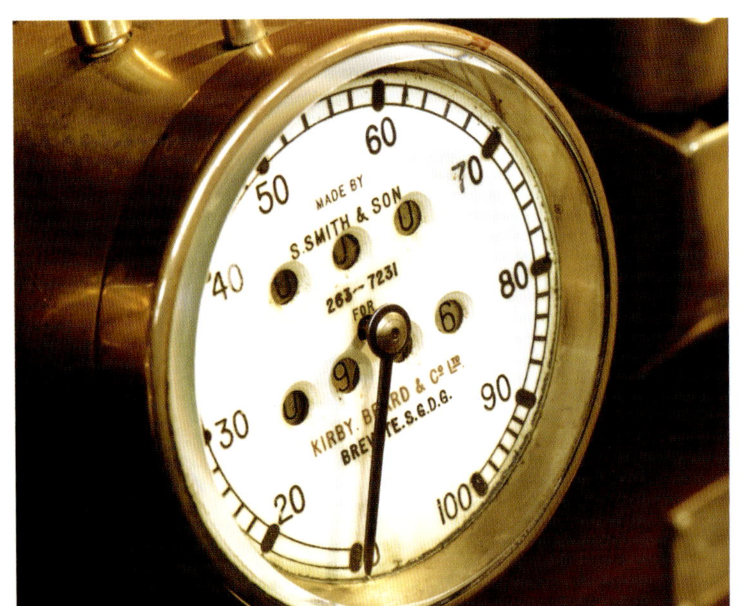

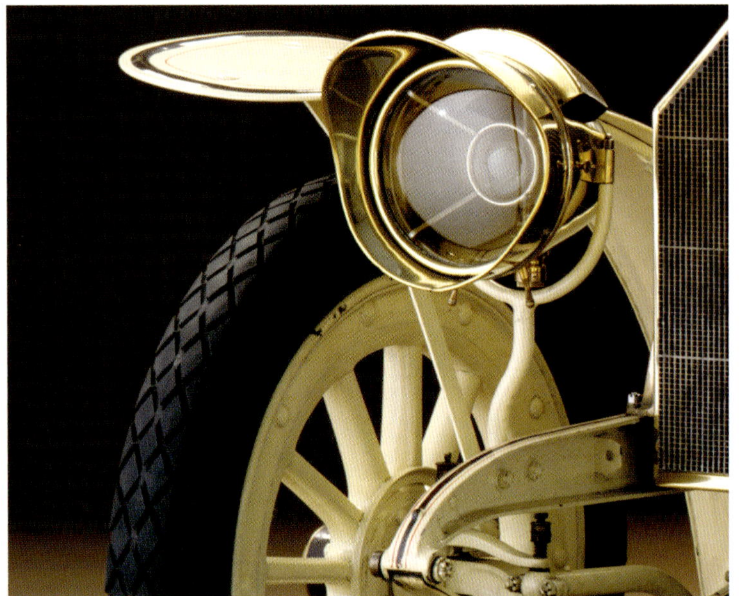

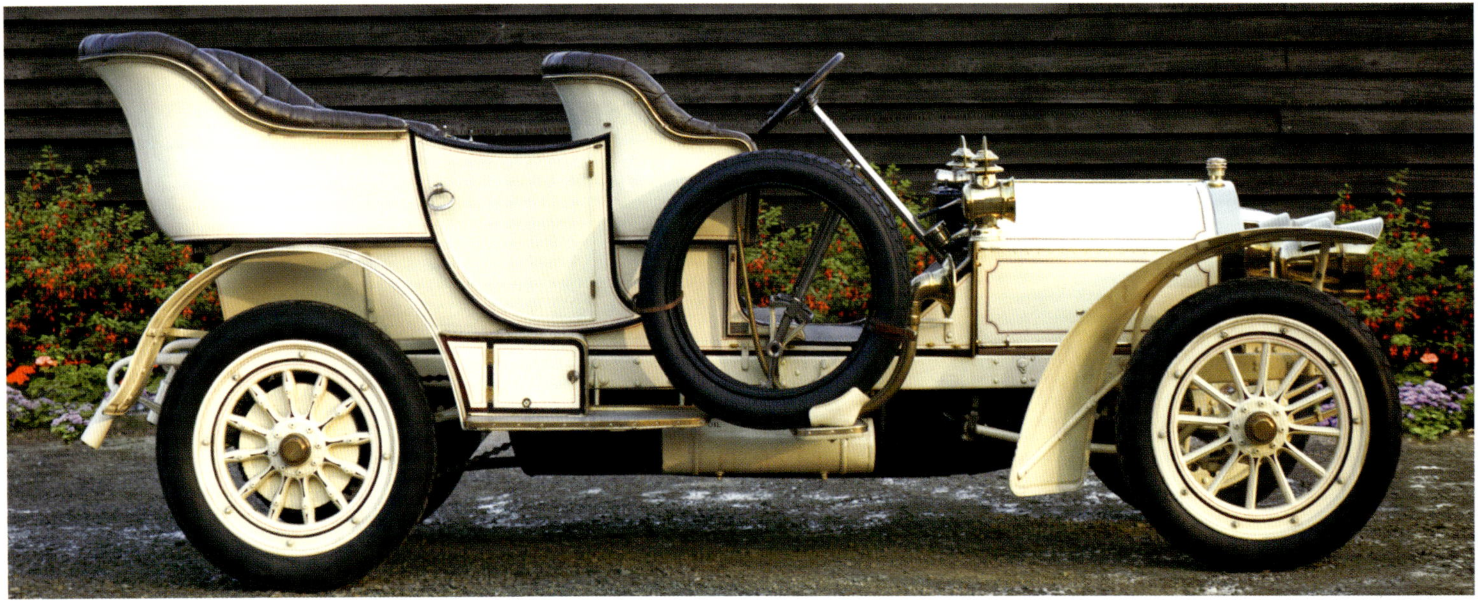

Messerschmitt FMR Tg 500 • Germany • 1958
OS - EV 65

OS
D 47

km
140
0
120
20
100
40
60
3 4 4 2
VDO

MG TC Midget • Great Britain • 1945
MG
RAC
OS TC 480

UNDO
MG
LEFT (NEAR) SIDE

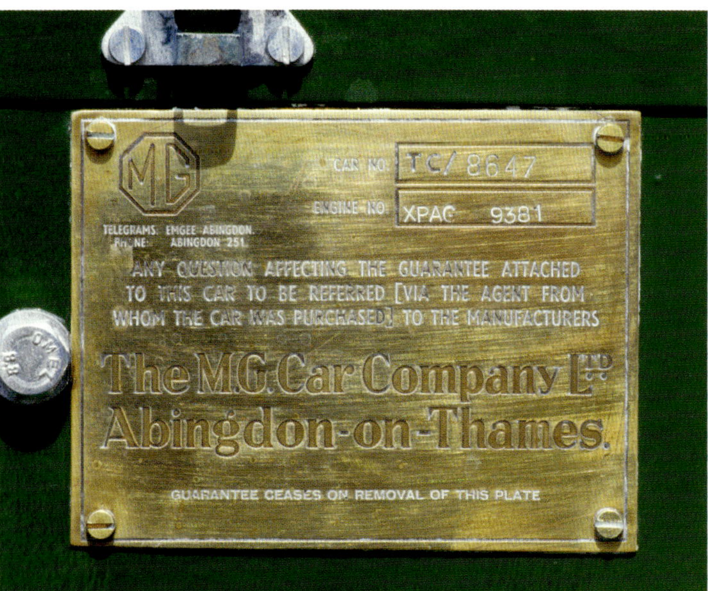
MG
CAR No TC/ 8647
ENGINE No XPAG 9381
TELEGRAMS: EMGEE ABINGDON.
PHONE: ABINGDON 251
ANY QUESTION AFFECTING THE GUARANTEE ATTACHED
TO THIS CAR TO BE REFERRED [VIA THE AGENT FROM
WHOM THE CAR WAS PURCHASED] TO THE MANUFACTURERS
The M.G. Car Company Ltd
Abingdon-on-Thames.
GUARANTEE CEASES ON REMOVAL OF THIS PLATE

MI NI 5065
D

M
M
BPE 868

BPE
868

NSU Ro 80 · Germany · 1967
OS·H 8080

Opel Kapitän • Germany • 1949

MS·KE 272

KAPITÄN

OPEL
MS - KE 272

Packard Hawk • USA • 1958
PACKARD
4354 PF

Pagani Zonda C 12 S • Italy • 2000

Panhard Dynamic Typ X76 • France • 1936

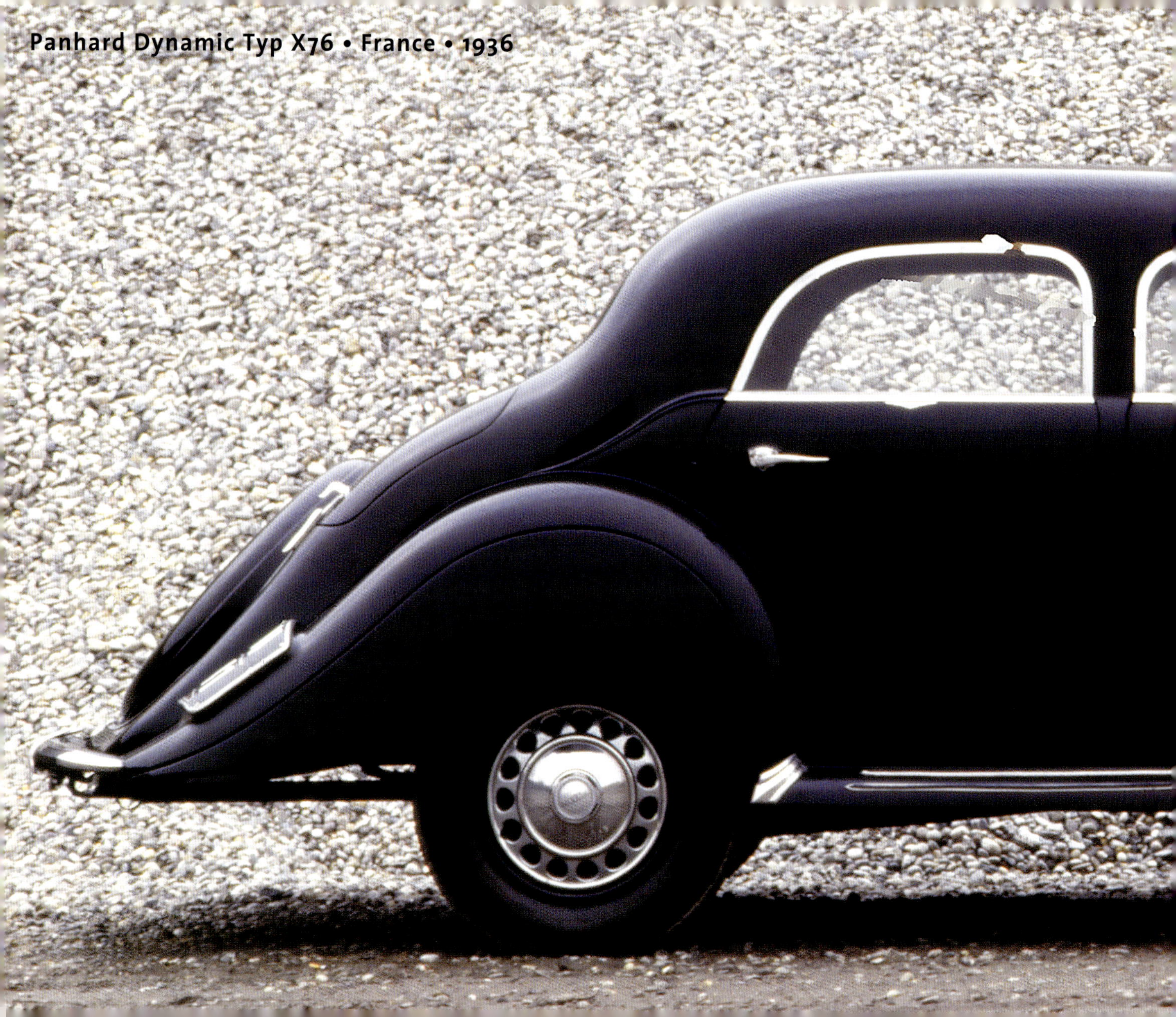

44
T41

44
T41

70 80 100 110
130
140
150
160

69 NEVADA
W1933

Plymouth P12 · USA · 1942

GT·JJ6

Plymouth

Porsche 356 C Cabriolet • Germany • 1963
OS·HR 16

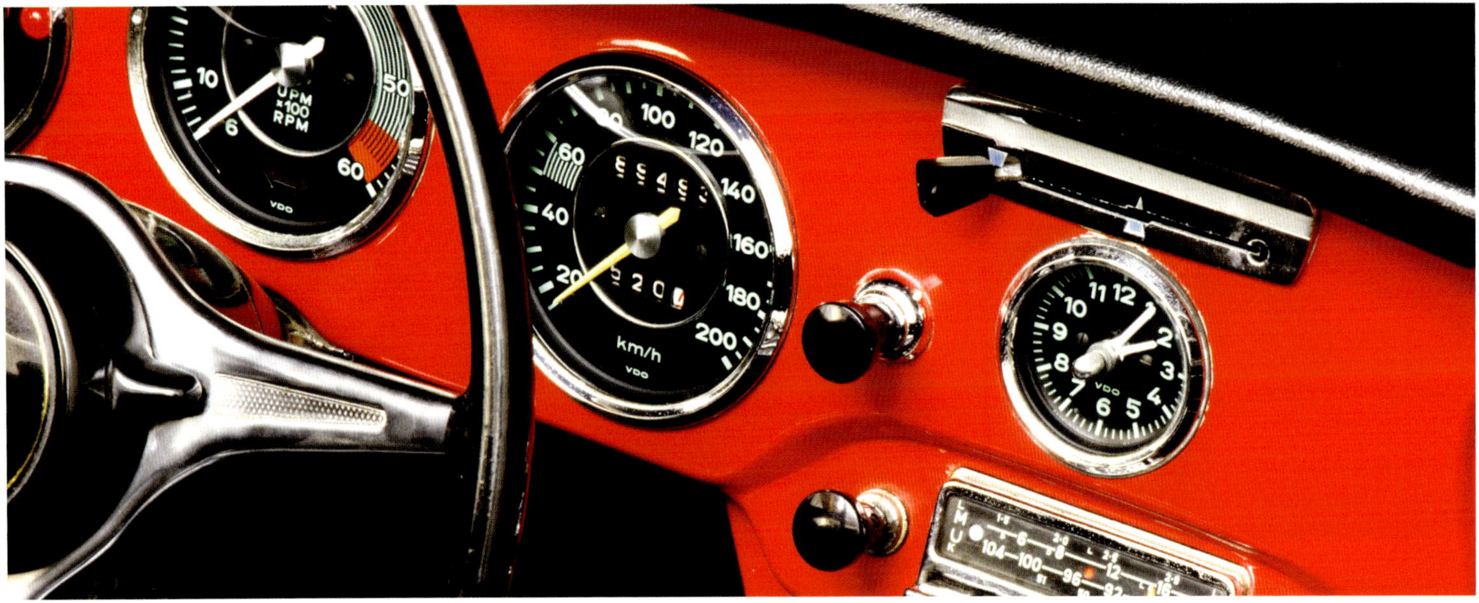
UPM
x100
RPM
VDO
km/h
VDO
VDO
PORSCHE
PORSCHE C
OS-HR 16

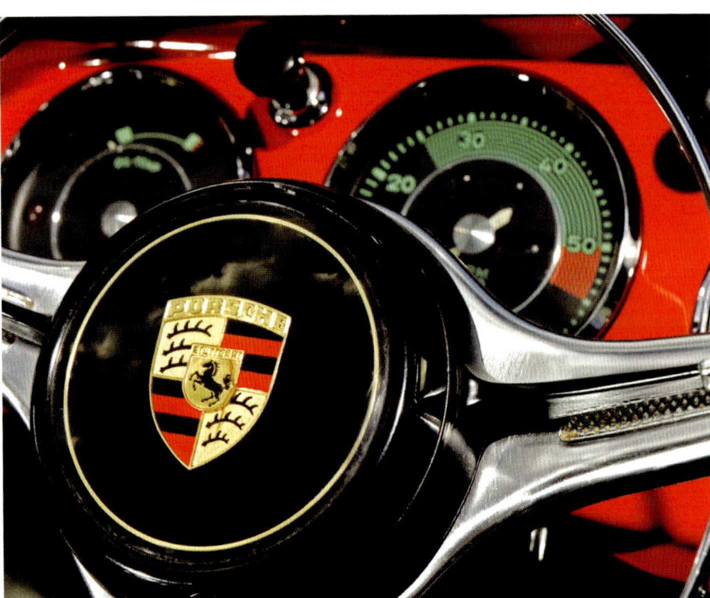

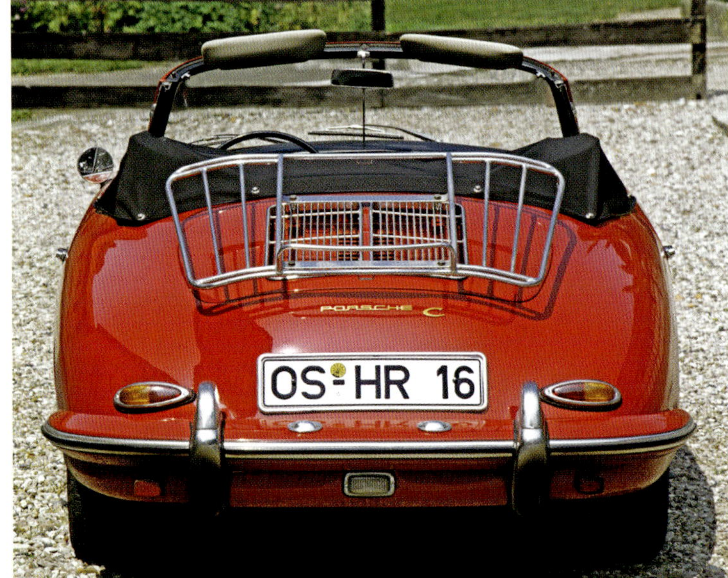

OS - JP 38

Porsche 904 GTS • Germany • 1963

GT3

338

Renault Type KJ Torpedo • France • 1924

PM·93?

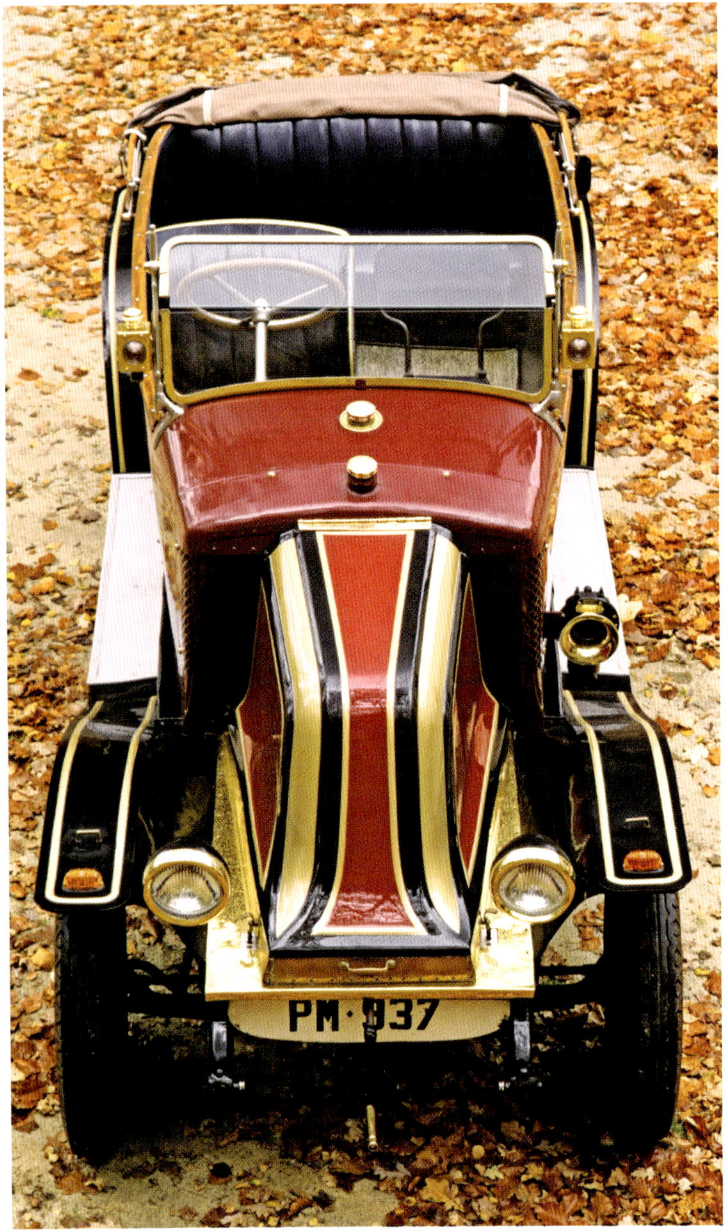
PM·937

GAZ O
AIR
MARCHE

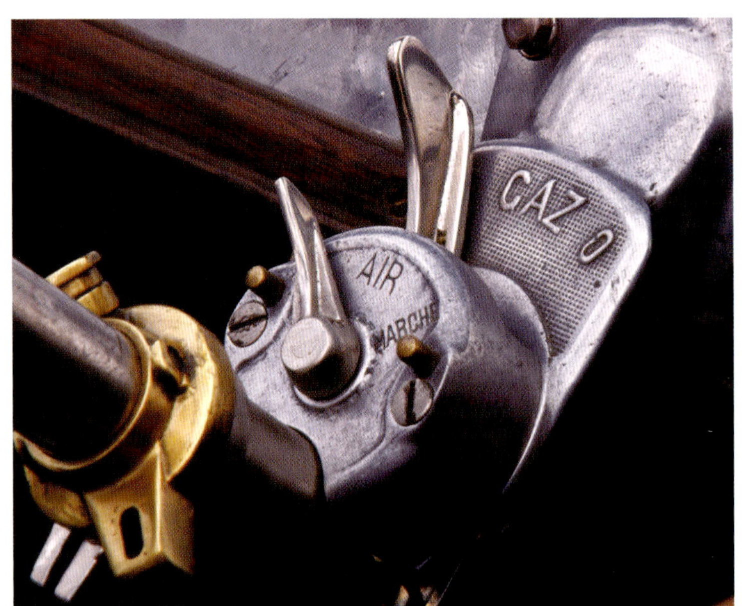

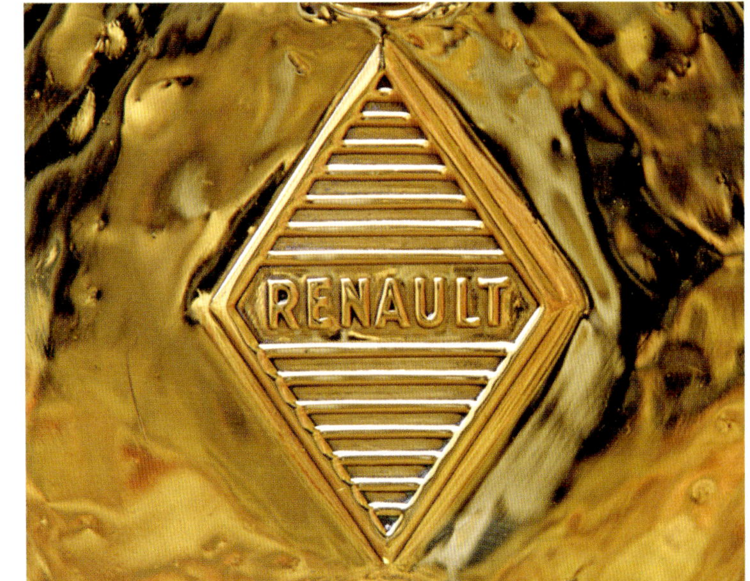

RENAULT

Rolls Royce Phantom II by Hooper • Great Britain • 1929

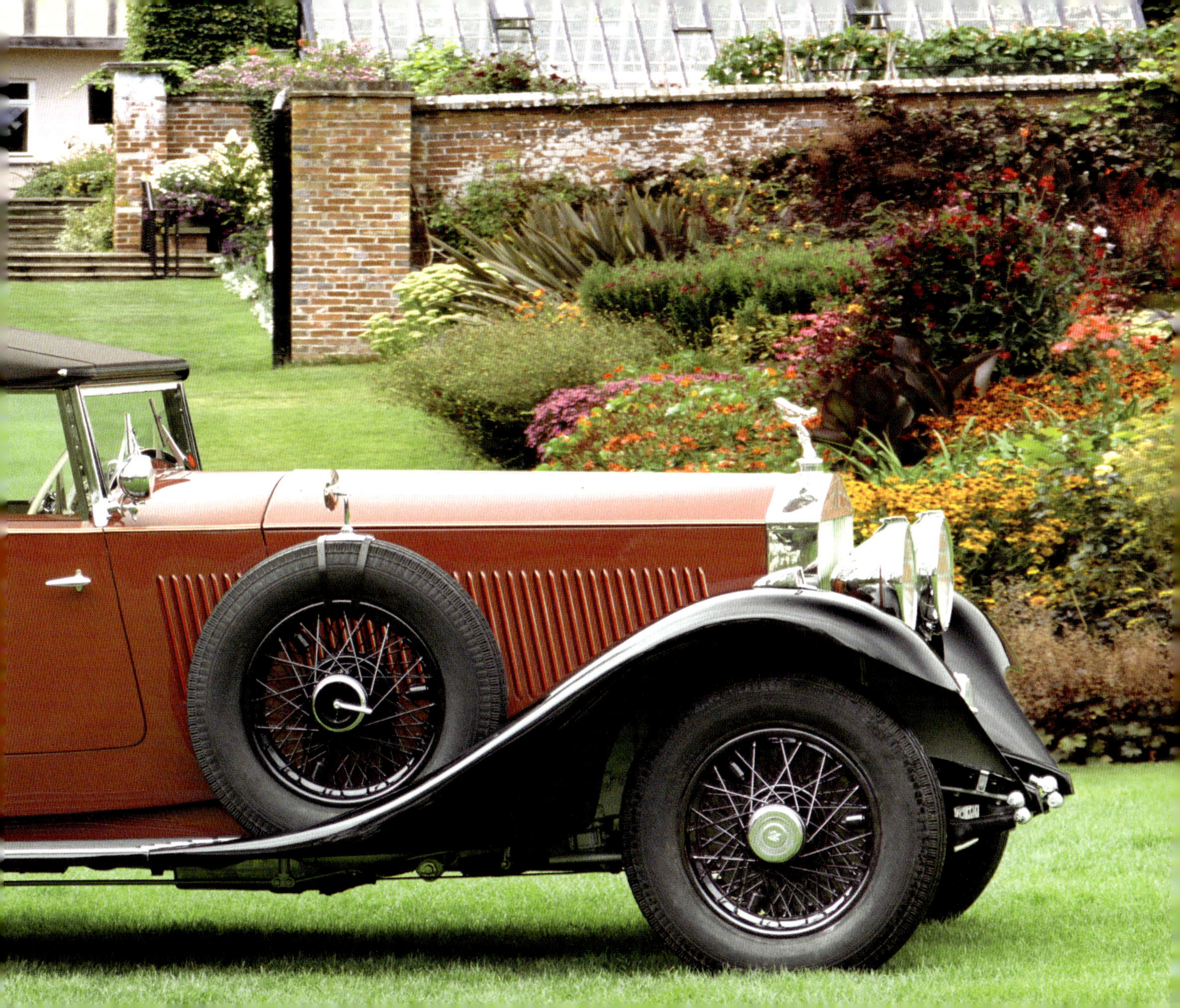

RR 3

ROLLS

Rolls Royce Phantom Drophead Coupé • Great Britain • 2007

POWER
RESERVE %
AIRBAG
LOW MED HIGH
AUTO

Talbot Lago Figoni & Falaschi Coupé • France • 1938

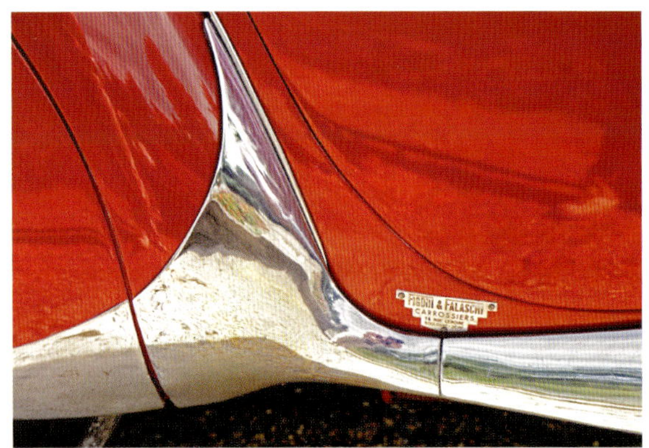

F
3745
PRINCIPAUTÉ DE MONACO
F

Tucker Torpedo • USA • 1948
CALIFORNIA
575 KIE
TUCKER 1948

Tucker
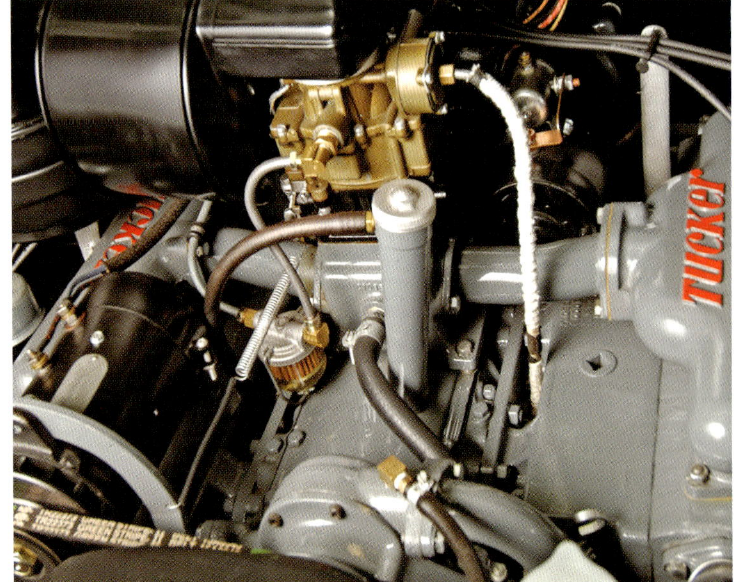
TUCKER
TUCKER

Tucker
CALIFORNIA
575 KIE
TUCKER 1948

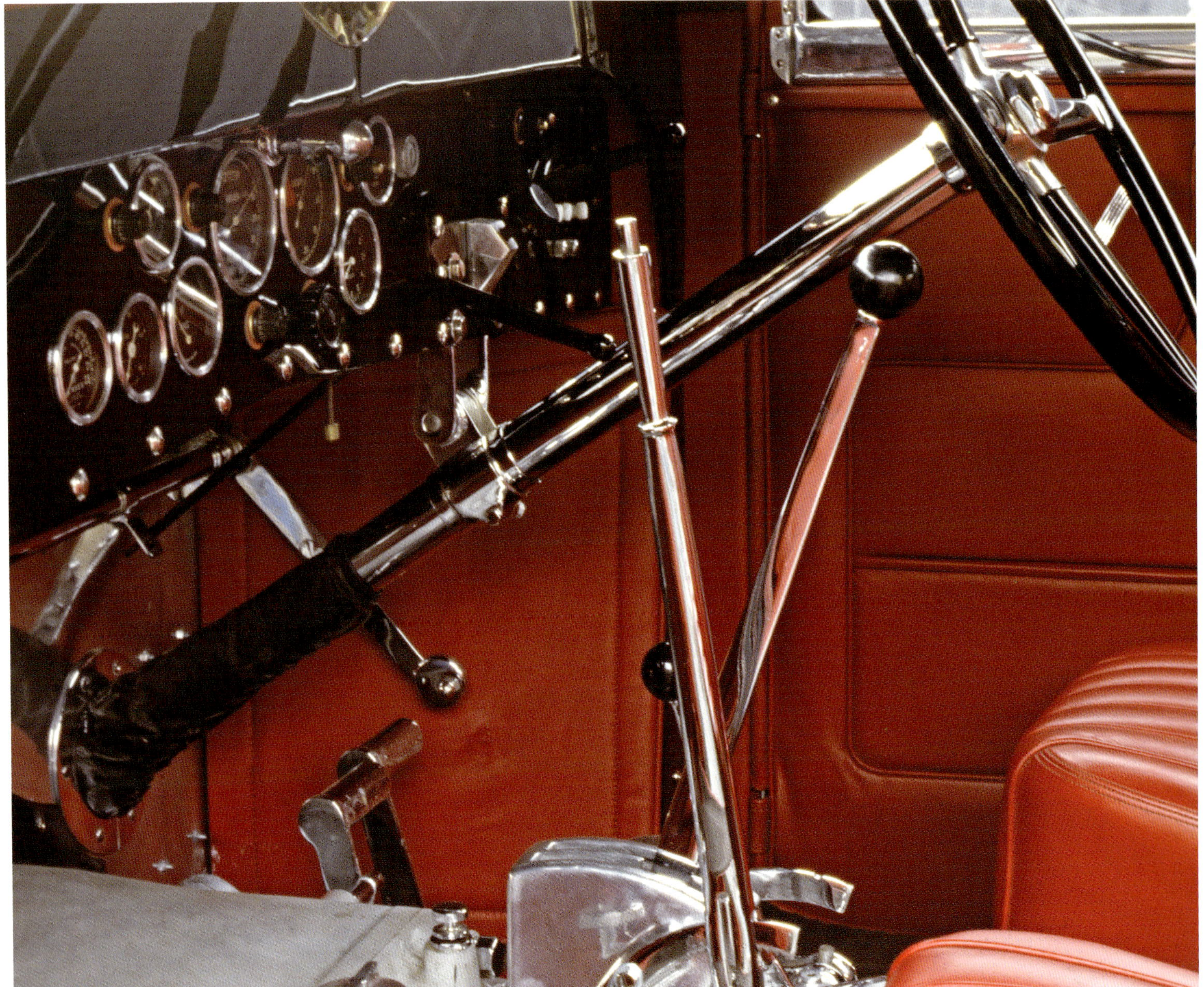

AVIONS

Volkswagen VW Käfer 1300 • Germany • 1965
URD 295J

20 MILLIONEN

URD 295 J

Volkswagen VW Karmann Ghia 1300 • Germany • 1965

HA-M 286

Wanderer W 25 K • Germany • 1936

W - 25 K

W - 25 K

°C
°C
160
140
120
100
80
60
40
20
0
5 1 6 0
5000
4500
4000
3500
3000
2500
2000
UMDR.
W
11 12 1
10 2
9 3
8 4
7

500
000
00
OEL
BENZIN
¼ ½ ¾ 4/4
WASSER
40 60 80
°C
°C

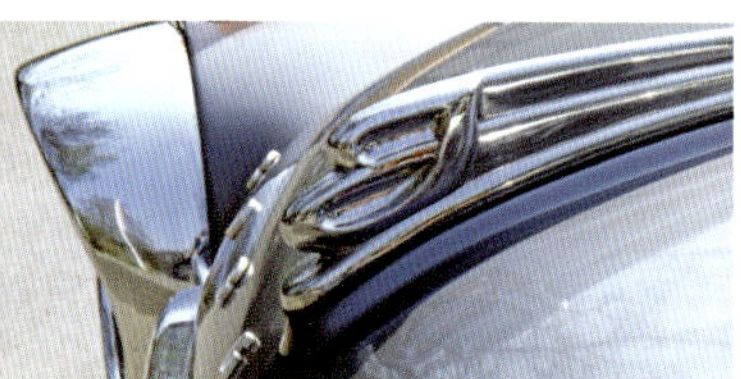